JUSTIFY

JUSTIFY

111 Days to Triple Crown Glory

Lenny Shulman

No part of this publication may be reproduced, stored in a retrieval system, or transmitted in any form by any means, electronic, mechanical, photocopying, or otherwise, without the prior written permission of the publisher, Triumph Books LLC, 814 North Franklin Street, Chicago, Illinois 60610.

Library of Congress Cataloging-in-Publication Data

Names: Shulman, Lenny, author.
Title: Justify : 111 days to Triple Crown glory / Lenny Shulman.
Description: Chicago, Illinois : Triumph Books, LLC, [2019]
Identifiers: LCCN 2018060689 | ISBN 9781629377018
Subjects: LCSH: Justify (Horse) | Race horses—United States-Biography. |
    Horse racing—United States. | Triple Crown (U.S. horse racing)
Classification: LCC SF355.J87 S58 2019 | DDC 798.40092/9—dc23
LC record available at https://lccn.loc.gov/2018060689

This book is available in quantity at special discounts for your group or organization. For further information, contact:
    Triumph Books LLC
    814 North Franklin Street
    Chicago, Illinois 60610
    (312) 337-0747
    www.triumphbooks.com

Printed in U.S.A.
ISBN: 978-1-62937-701-8
Design by Patricia Frey
Photos courtesy of AP Images unless otherwise indicated

CONTENTS

FOREWORD

YOU ARE ABOUT TO EMBARK ON A JOURNEY UNLIKE ANYTHING ever seen in Thoroughbred racing. It is a whirlwind journey that left greatness not to the stat sheet, but to the imagination, much like an unfinished Mozart concerto or a Degas pastel that was finished quickly in order to capture the essence of his subject.

Justify was his own subject and was able to capture his essence in only 111 days. Whether unfinished or not, it was a masterpiece that changed the course of racing history.

What Justify accomplished in some three and a half months during arguably the most meteoric rise in racing history is unprecedented. He will always be remembered as the horse who continually rewrote the history books, defying several significant historical trends of more than 100 years, including the much publicized "Apollo Curse," becoming the first horse in 136 years to win the Kentucky Derby without having raced as a 2-year-old. To accomplish that off only three lifetime starts and then go on to sweep the Triple Crown is something we likely will never see again. And to do it after running the fastest fractions ever by a Kentucky Derby winner elevated him into a realm of his own.

Most horses with such little racing foundation would need time to recover from such an arduous task, but he came right back in two weeks, despite exiting the Derby with a bruised foot, and outdueled the previous year's 2-year-old champion and Kentucky Derby runner-up, Good Magic, putting him away after racing eyeball to eyeball from the start. His Preakness victory proved to be a metaphor for his career, as he emerged from the dense fog like some ghostly shroud, with his white silks and white face. The Pimlico stretch, like that year's Derby trail, was a blank canvas, with everyone waiting anxiously for that one special image to appear from seemingly out of nowhere.

His Belmont Stakes victory, just 111 days after his career debut, provided a curtain call to rival opening night of *Hamilton* on Broadway. Every single person in the audience knew they had witnessed history being made.

To put everything in proper perspective, Justify accomplished something in 16 weeks that it took all the previous Triple Crown winners an average of 11 months to accomplish.

And he did it racing on three fast tracks, two sloppy tracks, and one muddy track, while winning his six races at six different distances, from seven furlongs to a mile and a half.

Never before had we seen a horse exhibit such recuperative powers at that early an age. Despite the rigorous grind he was put through, Justify showed no ill effects, bouncing out of each race like a fresh horse; seemingly stronger than the race before. From his victory in the Santa Anita Derby to his Triple Crown sweep in the Belmont Stakes, he lost a total of three pounds. That is unheard of, especially for a 1,260-pound horse.

But in many cases, venturing into uncharted waters with a young, inexperienced horse and asking so much of those spindly legs comes with a price, and the Belmont was the last racing fans would see of Justify, which brings up the subject of his legacy. In addition to what he accomplished in what seemed a blink of the eye, he showed us that there is nothing unattainable, regardless of what history tells us. He made us realize that there no longer are worlds that cannot be conquered. He taught us that history books are not merely rule books and guidelines of how things should be done, but that there are always new pages to be written, as implausible as they may seem.

Justify proved that a great horse didn't need to win by large margins or break track records. He won under any conditions, at any racetrack, at any distance, and against all competition, and he did it without having a breather and with virtually no racing foundation under him. And, because of his whirlwind career, his grand appearance, and his will to win, he captured the public's heart and imagination, and was able to step out of the daunting shadow cast by American Pharoah.

There are a number of factors that determine how an individual is treated in the history books and how he or she will be remembered by future generations. There are the track and world records set by Secretariat, Dr. Fager, and Swaps. There are the staggering weights carried by Forego, Kelso, Discovery, Exterminator, and, again, Dr. Fager. There is the dominance over a long period of time by warriors such as John Henry, Kelso, and Exterminator. There are those rare iconic figures who transcend the Sport of Kings and become part of our culture, such as Man o' War, Secretariat, and Seabiscuit. And, finally, there is the most exclusive of clubs, the 13 Triple Crown winners.

Although Justify belongs only in the final category, he will forever be remembered as the horse who established his own niche in the history books by changing the fabric of the sport. In short, he was a true revolutionary, accomplishing feats never believed possible in such a short period of time. By defying numerous historical trends, he no doubt altered the way future horses are trained in preparation for the classics.

In the pages that follow, you will be taken behind the scenes and meet the people and witness the events that set this extraordinary machine in motion. Those who bred him, sold him, purchased him, broke him, prepped him, trained him, owned him, and now stand him at stud, formed a continuous chain, each with the knowledge and gratification that they helped move this unique athlete along toward his place in history.

The legendary British and Irish race-caller Sir Peter O'Sullevan used to say whenever he witnessed a truly remarkable performance by a special racehorse, "What manner of horse is this?"

In the case of Justify, the answer to that question, again, is something left to the imagination.

Steve Haskin is a longtime Turf writer who has covered horse racing for 42 years and the Kentucky Derby/Triple Crown for 32 years. He has written six books on the sport, won numerous awards including six Red Smith Awards for his Kentucky Derby coverage, and in 2016 was elected to the National Museum of Racing's Hall of Fame Media Roll of Honor.

INTRODUCTION

HORSE RACING, MORE THAN ANY OTHER SPORT, EMBRACES THE
inevitable comparison of heroes from different eras. Perhaps it is
because of the importance of the pedigrees of the athletes, amassed
over decades of carefully nourished bloodlines; or, simply, maybe
it is the need for a good argument among fans who regularly back
their opinions with money.

Was Secretariat superior to Man o' War? Could Affirmed
compete with Citation? Was Seattle Slew the equal of American
Pharoah? Perhaps debates are not supposed to result in defini-
tive answers; maybe their appeal is in the illusion that through
opinion, we can break the code and think what we believe is
the ultimate truth, and that we can then somehow know the
unknowable.

The comet that streaked across the Thoroughbred racing
world in 2018 is destined to become one of the most controversial unanswered questions in the sport's annals. This is what we
know about the 3-year-old colt Justify: he accomplished more in
less time than any other Thoroughbred in U.S. racing history.
He rewrote various pages of the record book. He is just the 13th

Triple Crown winner in the 100 years since the Kentucky Derby, Preakness, and Belmont Stakes have been grouped together as classic races; and only the second horse to win the Triple Crown while undefeated and also the first Triple Crown winner to retire undefeated.

But Justify's race career will forever be remembered for two outstanding characteristics, one positive, the other less so: his brilliance, and the brevity of his time in competition. Every horseman who came in contact with him recognized in short order his superior ability. Justify went through each level of his training with an ease that defied the task at hand. Not only was he growing into a perfect racehorse before the eyes of his handlers, his superior intellect and mentality for his job allowed him to blossom free of the roadblocks that stop so many racehorses in their tracks.

The breeders and farm managers who guide these hot-blooded Thoroughbreds through their formative years to a person claim that their charges spend every day thinking up ways to injure themselves, and often succeed. And that is on farms, in pristine pastures, far from the rigors of racing. Justify handled everything thrown at him like he was doing it as an older horse for the 10th time instead of as a 3-year-old for the first. Flying to new racetracks; acclimating to new surroundings; handling throngs of fans and media whenever he left his barn; performing in front of tens of thousands of screaming patrons; racing against ever more challenging competition and over greater distances of ground. Nothing fazed this young racehorse, who captured the Triple Crown in June of his 3-year-old season despite not having raced at 2.

In fact, he became the first horse since Apollo in 1882 to win the Kentucky Derby without benefit of a race as a 2-year-old. For decades, owners would badger their trainers to hurry up and start a 2-year-old before the calendar turned, believing they had no shot to win the Kentucky Derby otherwise. Horses not yet ready to run would thus be forced into racing to try to keep their owners' Derby dreams alive. Although Justify's is not a template likely to fall into favor with coming generations of horsemen and young horses, he proved that what was thought to be impossible was, in fact, doable.

Analytics have been applied to horse racing long before coming into favor in other major sports, again fueled by its long association with gambling. Various speed figures and sheet numbers have been assigned by different purveyors to every race-horse for decades before the arrival of Justify. While performances can be quantified in an attempt to predict the future, they cannot definitively do so. Very few have beaten this game at the betting windows, mainly because they are attempting to presage the efforts of living, breathing horses who have daily ups and downs, aches and pains, and possess hearts that can either carry them to great glory or fail to care whether they finish a race first or fourth.

Some of the sport's patrons utilize their eyeballs to try and determine the health and well-being of a horse on any given day. How is the horse's coat? His demeanor? His behavior? On looks, as on the racetrack, Justify never failed. He is a chestnut beauty whose color shades toward the red made famous by the acknowledged greatest racehorses of the past century, Man o' War and Secretariat, both known as "Big Red" in their day.

Certain horses radiate a striking presence in whatever they do. Walking around their barn, heading to the racetrack at dawn to train, or circling a saddling paddock before a race, eyes are drawn to them. Justify is one of these. He fills your vision and exudes power, muscles rippling off his shoulders and through his powerful hind end, what horsemen refer to as "the motor." He is taller than Secretariat though not as broad through his girth, and one would have to search long and hard to find a better representative of the Thoroughbred breed.

Racing, though, is not a beauty pageant. Every year at Thoroughbred sales, buyers sign tickets agreeing to pay hundreds of thousands, if not millions, of dollars for outstanding physical specimens who turn out not to be able to run any faster than their owners. On the other hand, an overweight, slothlike-looking horse bereft of any obvious beauty like Seattle Slew can be bought for $17,000 and ultimately change his owners' lives and the Thoroughbred industry forever.

It turns out Justify has it all: the looks and the talent. He proves to be able to run faster and over longer distances than any other of his generation. He can run over ground wet and dry, and over four different racetracks without a blip. He can give his classmates months-long head starts in racing experience and make up the gap with consummate ease. He can go immediately to the lead when the starting gates open, or sit just behind the pacesetter, keeping his energy in reserve without wasting a drop on anxiety.

Thoroughbreds are a breed beset by physiognomy that seems a God-given joke. Twelve-hundred-pound animals asked to be performance athletes running on legs impossibly spindly for the task at hand. Regularly their training is interrupted by setbacks, be they the growing pains of young horses or specific bone, joint, and tendon problems that are byproducts of constant impact in motion. No matter how safe racetracks are made or how carefully training regimens are plotted, injuries are a constant.

Justify, who is late to mature and grow into his large frame for the task at hand—becoming a viable racehorse—is forced to play catch-up from the day he is shipped to the racetrack to begin training. He is so tardy to come to hand that under normal cir-cumstances his connections would not even begin to dream that he will progress quickly enough to compete in the Triple Crown races. To do so, he would not be able to afford even one day of missed training to any of the myriad maladies that beset the breed. One may as well wish for the sun to rise in the West as to believe a Thoroughbred in training can go seven months without some sort of setback. With Justify, though, the sun somehow does rise in the West, and the impossible comes to pass.

Every breeder who sells a racehorse knows how crucial it is for that horse to wind up in the hands of a trainer who can get the best out of him. When a horse excels on the track, his family increases in value, and the breeder is thus able, theoretically, based on sound conformation, to sell younger brothers and sisters of the good racer for more money. Justify's breeder, John Gunther, knows he's hit the jackpot when Justify winds up in the hands of trainer Bob Baffert in California.

Baffert is the top trainer of his generation when it comes to developing young horses for the Triple Crown races and has moved himself into the conversation of greatest Thoroughbred trainer of all time. He begins the 2018 season two wins behind his hero, D. Wayne Lukas, for the most wins ever in Triple Crown races. Justify's Triple Crown sweep will vault Baffert into the top spot on that list and make him just the second trainer in history to win two Triple Crowns.

We all come, at one point or another, to realize that none of our heroes are perfect. Childhood worship and fascination give way, bit by bit, to the reality that Santa Claus doesn't come down the chimney and that athletes legendary on the field of battle might be flawed off it. Justify's flaw, through no fault of his own, is that he is a product of his times. Horse racing today has passed from the time of monarchs and industrialists boasting that "My horse is faster than yours" to what is known today as the commercial era, where horses are sold instead of kept. They are commodities more than they are family.

The great dynasties that for generations bred and raced their own stock are 99 percent gone by 2018. Today horses are bred and raised to be sold at market for top dollar to owners seeking gratification and riches from their race records, and a possible sale as a breeding animal down the road. While the purse money available in racing has remained stagnant and does not keep pace with the costs and expenses needed to buy and train a racehorse, the real money has shifted to the breeding side of the industry. Specifically, those who own a top male racehorse can either sell him to a major breeding farm outright or retain an interest in him. The right horse from the right family with the right race record can turn into an equine cash register. Mare owners who seek the service of a top stud horse are asked to pony up $100,000, $200,000, or even $300,000 to have their mare impregnated by the desired stallion. In one breeding season, which stretches in the U.S. from mid-February until the end of June, a desirable stallion can "cover" up to 300 mares, with perhaps 225 to 250 of those mares getting in foal. You needn't be a mathematician to conclude that such a top stallion is worth far more than he would be as a racehorse.

Justify comes to prominence in this era of commercial interests and modern-day mergers and acquisitions. The list of his owners as a racehorse and the evolving roster of those with interest in him as a stallion prospect require a scorecard. So when he is beset by a minor injury after winning the Triple Crown, instead of giving him a few months' rest and resuming his racing career, his ownership entities decide it is far less risky to retire him, sparing further insurance premiums and any potential future chinks in his reputation should he fail to continue racing at the level at which he left off.

As an undefeated Triple Crown champion from a nice female family and by a proven stallion who died young, Justify is sure to be in demand as a sire. Such an early retirement, though, never sits well with the fans of horse racing, who want to see their heroes compete and not be whisked away while still in their prime. And Justify's place in history will forever be open to debate, his obvious brilliance filtered through the brevity of his six-race career. Where can one place Justify in historical context? What weight to assign his accomplishments through the small window in which he thrilled us?

Imagine Michael Jordan or LeBron James scoring 50 points per game in their rookie seasons, leading their teams to NBA championships, and then retiring. Babe Ruth hitting 60 home runs as a rookie, with nobody else hitting more than 10, and then leaving baseball. Joe Montana or Tom Brady throwing six touchdown passes as rookies in the Super Bowl leading their teams to victory, and then passing from the scene.

That will forever be the mystery surrounding Justify. The last hurdle to be cleared by phenomenal 3-year-olds is their ability to compete against older horses, tests which come in the waning months of their 3-year-old season. And then, of course, comes their subsequent record as an older horse, and whether they can pass the test of maintaining their form over time while vanquishing new challengers. These are questions that Justify will never answer. The possibilities will be debated, and opinions stated as fact, but that is as far along the path of certainty as we will travel concerning him.

Racing fans are a funny breed. Some are drawn strictly to the gambling aspect of the sport; others by the beauty of the Thoroughbred. There are animal lovers and speed lovers; people who ride horses and people who are afraid to get close to them. Many irrationally hold the innocent horse culpable for the deeds of its connections. If we don't like a certain jockey, we can't like the horse he is riding. If we find an owner to be boorish or condescending or too rich or too ambitious, we can't brook the deeds of his or her horses. If we find a trainer too brash or too successful or suspect he or she is playing too loose with medicating their horses, we downplay any accomplishments of the runners in their care.

Human nature, perhaps. Most of us are prone, in one form or another, to this guilt by association. Our vision is distorted by these prisms, our views culled together based on various deflections no more real than a funhouse mirror. Justify will prove to be more susceptible to such distortions than any other great horse who came before him.

Runaway prices in the aftermath of the Great Recession of the late 2000s have seen all but the wealthiest owners in the game forming partnerships to spread risk when bidding competitively on top lots at Thoroughbred auctions. The chance of a Mom and Pop horse rising from oblivion to superstardom grows dimmer by the year.

On one level, the absence of horses borne of such romance, and the stories that surround their rags-to-riches tales, leave us unfulfilled in our preference for the underdog. Can we find enough satisfaction reveling in the accomplishments, in the pure athletic feats of these magnificent beings, without concerning ourselves with all else swirling around them? It is not easy, for we have far many more faults than do the Thoroughbreds who entertain us.

Justify may be the most brilliant racehorse to grace our presence since the Golden Age of the 1970s when Secretariat, Seattle Slew, Affirmed, and Alydar came to us in such close succession. He was near-perfection in motion from the time he first crashed into our consciousness. His moment with us was fleeting, but that should not diminish his accomplishments. We can acknowledge simply that it took him less time than any other to grab our attention and fascinate us with his pure talent.

JUSTIFY

1

ON HISTORY'S DOORSTEP

THE GRANDSTAND AT BELMONT PARK RUNS A QUARTER-MILE long, rebuilt in the 1960s to accommodate tens of thousands who regularly turned out on Saturday afternoons to see superstar racehorses like Kelso, Dr. Fager, Buckpasser, and Damascus ply their trade of running freely, as long and as fast as their legs could carry them.

When the grandstand filled on June 9, 2018, however, it was far more an exception than a regular occurrence. Today, live attendance at the racetrack is no longer necessary, or even preferred. Television and mobile devices beam the action to fans sitting comfortably on living room sofas; and players can gamble from the beach, mountains, or anywhere else they'd like to spend their weekends, by simply tapping on their phones.

But on this spring day 90,000-plus cram the grand old lady on the New York City/Long Island border because of the promise of a Triple Crown champion. Back behind the grandstand in the saddling paddock, circling under a 200-year-old Japanese white pine tree that was once part of the estate of noted New York attorney William DeForest Manice, is a 1,260-pound Thoroughbred named Justify whose copper coat is defined by inlets of rippling muscles off his shoulders and hindquarters. He has just been fitted with a tiny saddle cinched around his robust girth, and even his nine opponents seem to keep a wary eye on this specimen as he parades among them, waiting for the signal to dispense with these preliminaries and finally get to work.

It is 6:30 of a warm late afternoon, and the general admission masses have moved from the backyard picnic area and the long betting lines to the racetrack apron, craning their necks to capture the 100-foot-wide expanse of rich sandy dirt that stretches before them. Some are alcohol-powered, here for a happening and a good time. Others are horse-crazy young girls of all ages now, and some are young or middle-age men whose fathers and grandfathers brought them here as kids, where they bonded and were instilled with a fascination in the way the majestic Thoroughbred fulfills his nature to run.

Above them, in the box seats, are the industry's current stakeholders, the folks who own the farms where mares graze in vast green fields and foals are conceived and raised, and where the choice few accomplished racehorses and most-productive studs go about the business of trying to replicate themselves. Here are the breeders who plan the matings; the owners who give over hundreds of thousands for a yearling on the pure gamble that he might be able to run, fast and sound, a year or two down the road. The ones with skin in the impending battle mix nervously among the dealmakers and the agents and the racetrack executives from around the world.

From the next level up, in the swell luxury of air-conditioned dining rooms, watch the scions of the game, their names recognizable going back half a century and more, whose great-grandparents started stables and bred their carefully cultivated mare families to the finest sires of the day, keeping their stock to race before the era of the commercial market. Their horses may not make it to the winner's circle with the regularity of days gone, but their influence hasn't waned, nor their ability to occupy the best perches.

On any day but this one, the good clubhouse seats on Belmont's third floor can be had by anyone giving over a $5 bill to upgrade from the grandstand. On a normal afternoon fans lounge about, their *Racing Forms* and tout sheets spread around on empty surrounding chairs, their feet up, lazily taking in the races that go off every 30 minutes. Most of those minutes are spent grousing to friends or geographically available strangers about jockey, horse, or trainer malfeasance that cost them their wagers on the previous race. Today, though, those chairs cost 500 bucks and are filled by well-heeled fans from across the country, come to the big city for a chance to witness history. Their disappointments are far more muted than those of the regular clientele, and there are significant others accompanying, many of whom have already this week shopped the fine stores of Manhattan, the unofficial trade-off for their partners' day at the races.

Perched on an overhang above all is the press box, a narrow piece of antiquity reached after navigating a long, steamy hallway. It was once the home of fedoras and cigarette smoke and hard-boiled wise guys banging out a living on typewriter keys and ribbon-stained sheets of white paper. Figuring their beat provided them good information, this gang nevertheless gave back a hefty percentage of their wages at the betting window. Today, laptops no bigger than a Manila folder sit on the long tables and the key-tapping is far quieter. What little smoking there is takes place up a flight of stairs out on the roof, and the graying leftovers from the last generation are outnumbered now by young women who bring a new and different energy of fandom to the enterprise of Turf writing. The more passionate have filtered down to ground level to bear witness to the unfolding main event, hanging on the rail and taking cell phone photos.

It is 15 minutes to post time, and great waves of noise ebb and flow from the ground-floor track apron to the levels above. Electricity shoots through the crowd, the sort felt before the opening bell of a top heavyweight championship fight or as the home team takes the field for Game 7 of the World Series. The anticipation, the excitement of the unknown, the chance that history will be forever written and witnessed in the minutes to come, elicits a buzz that cuts clear up through the rafters, as the greatest city in the world hosts yet another signature event.

This business of the Triple Crown carries extra gravity because its potential occurrence is irregular. Barring labor unrest or owner lockouts, the top team sports hold their championship games annually. Horse racing's ultimate day, however, is predicated on one horse winning the first two legs of the classics, the Kentucky Derby and the Preakness Stakes, before he can run for the Triple Crown in the Belmont Stakes. Before the great Secretariat came along in 1973, 25 years had elapsed since the Triple Crown was captured by Citation in 1948. And since Affirmed turned the triple in 1978 by fending off Alydar in the final strides of their mile-and-a-half battle in the Belmont, fully 37 years passed—including 13 failures by Derby/Preakness winners to complete the triple here at Belmont—before American Pharoah set off a full-blown hullabaloo by winning the Triple Crown in 2015.

Supply and demand. On average, the Triple Crown has been won once per decade over the past century. It is the difference between watching an annual Fourth of July fireworks show and a once-a-decade meteor shower. Anticipation is heightened; nerves shoot through the assembled; no one wants to sit down.

The public-address system crackles with an announcement: "The New York Racing Association is proud to present…" The rest of the words are obscured both by outdated speakers and by a crease of noise that bounces off the walls of the giant grandstand. Strains of Frank Sinatra bellowing about "wanting to be a part of it" play over the faulty sound system, and all eyes turn to the action down near the tunnel that connects the saddling paddock to the racing surface. An outrider in black helmet and red vest and his mount slowly make their way toward the racetrack. Immediately behind them is the gleaming chestnut beauty seeking to make history today.

Having drawn the number 1 post in this field of 10 horses, Justify in every way leads the procession out onto the racetrack. His presence, with the Hall of Fame rider Mike Smith aboard him wearing the red silks with yellow stars of the China Horse Club (one of four ownership entities with a piece of the undefeated colt), brings a riptide roar from the assembled, which catches a first glimpse of him in staggered time depending on their vantage point. A historically inexperienced horse to be in this position, Justify, as he has all spring, remains aloof from the cacophony raining down upon him. He is a magnificent specimen of a Thoroughbred—his long body built for speed, a lengthy stride, power, and stamina; his ears straight up taking in the entirety of the scene; a brilliant white blaze narrowing between his eyes before broadening back up higher on his forehead. In any grouping of horses, he is a standout. Accompanied by a pony, he turns left up the racetrack toward the head of the stretch to begin the post parade, the anticipation of which produces another full-throated shower of cheers.

For interpreters of body language, Justify is providing ample hints that this, like his previous five races, will be his day.

Through the tests of the Derby and the Preakness, he has maintained his weight and increased his fitness. Such rigors, the first two races occurring just two weeks apart, have ruined many top horses who fail to repeat their Derby triumph. They are derailed by the energy expended or the travel from their home bases or their failure to acclimate, new situations falling outside their comfort level. These Thoroughbreds are hot-blooded, and they can go wrong at the smallest change in their routine. Anything out of place can cause them to fret and worry.

In addition to his massive stride and perfect conformation, Justify has the mental chops of a wise old warrior. Although his first foray into battle at the racetrack came just 111 days ago, he has handled a radically condensed schedule without turning a hair. After running through boggy, sloppy racing surfaces in the Derby and Preakness, perhaps he is thinking, as he walks over the sandy surface at Belmont Park, that he is finally getting to run on a dry track today, eliminating yet another variable in his pursuit of immortality.

"Here is the field for the Belmont Stakes. Number 1, Justify…" All else over the public-address is drowned out as the crowd whips itself into a frenzy at the mention of his name. The connections of his opponents are less impressed. Justify's margin of victory at the Preakness was decreasing with each mud-filled stride through the fog and muck. Surely his lack of a foundation from not having raced as a 2-year-old was catching up to him, according to those not yet convinced. And with the marathon 1½-mile Belmont lurking, that shortage of seasoning was bound to run him straight into a brick wall in New York, as it had so many others before him.

Only four had challenged Secretariat and Affirmed in the Belmont Stakes, while seven chose to do battle with Seattle Slew as he tried for the 1977 Triple Crown. But horsemen are lining up to take a crack at Justify as if the racing office was giving away free Caribbean vacations to all who entered. Justify, seeking to become just the second horse to win the Triple Crown while undefeated, is being looked upon as a freak show more than as a finished production. The gamblers are believers, betting him down to below even-money odds as the favorite. But the other owners and trainers have visions of sugar plums and that diminishing winning margin of the Preakness dancing in their heads, and each wants to go down in history as the spoiler, the defiler of Justify's perfect record.

As the starting gate is moved into position in front of the grandstand and just before the finish line—a mile and a half being one circuit of the gargantuan Belmont dirt track—Smith jogs Justify up the stretch and around the huge, gradual bend of the turn onto the backstretch, warming him up for the work at hand. Horse races are puzzles, as bettors try to piece together the strategy of each jockey and horse depending on their running style. Which will flash early speed and try to go to the front, which will try to find a position in mid-pack, and which will drop back toward the rear and make their run late in the proceedings?

Justify's speed is no secret. He's run on or close to the lead in all his races, having sat second in the Kentucky Derby waiting for a suicide frontrunner to empty his tank before assuming command. In the Preakness he showed the field his tail right off jump street. Here, from the inside post position, he would want to start alertly so as not to get boxed in by horses to his outside, whose jockeys would be only too happy to seal him off down at the rail and deny him running room. Everyone knew Justify would try for the lead in the Belmont. But would anyone else be able to do anything about it?

Warm-ups complete, the 10 Belmont starters begin their walk back down the stretch. "The horses are approaching the starting gate…" The three-week wait from the Preakness to the Belmont is finally at its conclusion, and the crowd voices its approval. The ponies who accompany the racers to keep them calm begin peeling away as assistant starters spring into action, each having a designated horse to lead into the starting gate. Justify is led first into his stall closest to the inner rail. The decibel level leaves all else a blur. The field loads quickly. Ninety-thousand patrons stand as one. At 6:50 PM, with the ringing of a bell and a loud thwack as the gates release, 10 heads shoot up the Belmont strip. Justify breaks inward for a step, and then instantly corrects course. He is in front in a matter of seconds, history beckoning a mile and a half farther down the strip.

CREATING A
DREAM

IT IS A TYPICALLY STICKY OHIO RIVER VALLEY JUNE DAY, relentless heat beaming mercilessly through heavy, still, wet air. The mercury reads mid-90s and standing outside is enough to cause sweat to seep through clothes. Well past 6:00 PM, the sun is still high in the sky in Louisville, Kentucky, on the western edge of the Eastern Time Zone. It is one week to the moment after Justify's run in the Belmont Stakes, and he is back at Churchill Downs, where his Triple Crown journey started, preparing to be paraded and celebrated out on the track where he sloshed through mud six weeks earlier to win the Kentucky Derby.

There is night racing at "The Downs" on this evening, and more than 20,000 patrons have shown up, many just to catch a glimpse of racing's new hero. At Barn 33, which is used by trainer Bob Baffert when he has horses running in the Derby and other prestigious races at Churchill Downs, Justify is led from his stall to a mat just outside. He is receiving a mini-bath, a washdown before he will be walked from the barn area around the race-track to the saddling paddock. There, he will be photographed by admirers before being led back out in front of the stands to the winner's circle to be hailed, and his connections given trophies for their Derby victory.

While accepting the cooling water across his chestnut body, Justify receives a visit from a familiar companion. Tanya Gunther, a lithe, sandy-haired woman, moves confidently to him and cradles his head in her arms. She plants a long kiss on top of his nose, lingers there a moment, and retreats back to the precious shade just inside the shedrow at the corner of the barn. Her shoulders begin to heave up and down, her head turned low. She is sobbing the joyful tears of seeing the embodiment of her wildest, most-far-fetched dream come to life in front of her wet eyes.

If he'd been born 1,000 miles to the south, perhaps John Gunther would have become a Hollywood character actor. His rugged features could well have made him a Jack Palance–type, riding horses over sagebrush-filled Western terrain either chasing villains or being one. But Gunther's involvement with horses would take a far different route up in western Canada.

His badlands came on the flats of Alberta, as did his education on self-sufficiency. Following the early death of his father, Gunther went to live on a farm owned by his aunt, who raised cattle, pigs, wheat, barley, and oats. His love affair with horses began there, with his fascination of the team that harrowed the fields. Following a family tradition, as a young man he worked the waterfront as a longshoreman, the piers conveniently located across the road from Hastings Park. Gunther spent weekends leaving behind part of his paycheck trying to unlock the puzzle of betting the horses. Amid the losses was one important gain—the hatching of a dream to one day own a Thoroughbred.

A different loss set Gunther on his primary career path. Sharing a beer-hall table near the docks with a group of stockbrokers, Gunther followed their tout and invested in a stock that landed belly up. Rather than lament his turn of fortune, Gunther decided to leave the unloading of ships to others and take the Canadian Securities Course to become a stockbroker himself. It was the move of a strong, self-made man, and today, 45 years associated with Leede Jones Gable, he is a senior partner in the firm.

Gunther early on bought a horse for a woman who would become his wife. Unknown to him, the mare was a Thoroughbred, and a friend eventually talked him into breeding her. Gunther raced her first foal, Pallascheck, who won four races for him and set him up for his life's avocation.

Not satisfied with the cheap local horses he was campaigning in Canada, Gunther began annually trekking to central Kentucky to upgrade his stock with a yearling or two. Instinctively, he decided in 1986 to buy into a Bluegrass farm named Glennwood, and within three years had bought out his partners in the 400-acre spread. The farm's main client for boarding mares was another Canadian, John Toffan, who had gotten lucky drilling a rich gold mine, and continued his good fortune with horses. Toffan owned such standout racers as multiple grade 1 winner Free House; Mane Minister, who finished third in all three Triple Crown races in 1991; and grade 1 winners Bien Bien and Pacific Squall.

As Gunther made himself into a highly successful stockbroker, quarterly earnings weren't the only numbers he was devouring. He immersed himself in horse-industry publications, studying pedigrees as well as the daily past performances, noting how top horses were bred. He used that information well and enjoyed the same good fortune as Toffan. Gunther bought mares at Kentucky auctions and established families at Glennwood that performed well as runners and then as producers.

"I've never used a bloodstock agent to buy a horse or a consignor to sell one," Gunther said with a laugh. These are highly specialized tasks, and it is unusual for one man to run all these aspects of his horse operation. "I did it myself by looking at a lot of horses over the years, and also getting lucky. Going back to the '70s, I've studied race results and pedigrees. My [stockbroker] partners are in Toronto and I'm in Vancouver, which works quite well. Apparently, they think I work every day."

Steve Irwin, a New York attorney, is a lifelong friend and business associate of Gunther's. "John has an uncanny ability to cut through façade," Irwin said. "He can walk into a room of strangers and know immediately who is real and who isn't; who can write a check and who can't. If he says, 'This is the deal,' then that is the deal. There's no monkeying around and trying to change this or that. He's a really right guy."

In the past 25 years, Gunther has bred 45 stakes winners, more than 20 of whom have won at the higher, graded level. His daughter, Tanya, grew up going to Hastings Park with her parents, falling in love with the morning visits to see the horses train. She rode ponies and then hunters and jumpers in her teens, becoming proficient enough at 16 to compete in the National Horse Show at Madison Square Garden. In the age-old parent's wish that their children have the benefits denied themselves, John Gunther made sure his daughter got off the farm to taste the outside world. Tanya earned a master's degree in finance from the London School of Business and has worked as an investment banker. While she still travels extensively, the call of the pastures remains strong in her, and she spends a substantial amount of time at Glennwood, overseeing every aspect of breeding and raising Thoroughbreds.

Although he possesses a foundation of decades of study, ultimately John Gunther employs a shoot-from-the-hip, gut instinct when buying potential broodmares and planning their subsequent matings. His daughter is more the analyst, giving over weeks and months to the study and research of pedigrees and the results of certain families matched with certain others. She often uses boxing metaphors when describing her discussions with her father over selecting stallions for their mares.

"I try to provide good ideas and advice while not letting my sensibilities get in the way of his vision," said Tanya. "It's a delicate balancing act at times. We do some sparring and we don't pull any punches. I can't repeat some of it; he and I will argue about certain things."

In 2005, John Gunther saw something in the chestnut mare Magical Illusion that caught his eye, and he bought her at auction for $425,000. Sent to the court of the Breeders' Cup Classic winner and very speedy racehorse Ghostzapper, Magical Illusion produced Stage Magic, a filly good enough to place in four stakes races in 2011 and earn $133,981 before being retired for broodmare duty at Glennwood.

In 2013, some sparring occurred when the Gunthers discussed a breeding partner for Stage Magic. Tanya had her eye on Scat Daddy as a solid value at a $30,000 stud fee. Her analysis of his numbers identified him as a potential breakout sire. Her father, however, saw Scat Daddy as a horse who was more proficient at producing racers who excelled on grass—and he was more interested in producing dirt runners. Father won, and Stage Magic was sent to Harlan's Holiday that year, with a deal struck for the subsequent season.

"He had to permit me to do the mating to Scat Daddy the following year," said Tanya. "We have negotiations like that."

The Gunthers were already having a great day on March 28, 2015. One horse they bred and raised, Tamarkuz, won the Godolphin Mile, a grade 1 event in Dubai; and another, Materiality, scored in the Florida Derby, an important grade 1 stepping-stone race for the Kentucky Derby. To win two such races in one day is a once-in-a-lifetime occurrence for operations far bigger than the Gunthers'. To do so from a band of less than two dozen broodmares is unheard of. So spirits were sky-high at Glennwood Farm when later that night Stage Magic foaled a strong, good-looking Scat Daddy colt.

"Along comes this colt while we were still trying to get our heads around the odds of having two horses bred and raised at Glennwood winning these prestigious races on opposite sides of the world on the same day," Tanya said.

Horsemen can be a superstitious lot and can see omens in every field of vision. The emotions of the moment were running high, and that special feeling stuck with Tanya Gunther.

"She said that we shouldn't sell that Scat Daddy foal because she felt something special was going on there that day," said her father. "It really spoke to her."

Horse farmers who tell you they knew a horse was going to be a star from birth are almost always engaging in hindsight hyperbole. About the best one can say about a foal or weanling (Thoroughbreds become yearlings on the January 1 after they are born) is that it is straightforward, which means it required no undue medical attention in its early days, rare enough when it comes to racehorses.

The Gunthers keep 20 broodmares at Glennwood. Certain years mares can be left "open," or not bred, while others may not carry their pregnancy to term. On average, perhaps 15 foals will be born and raised in a typical year, and the Scat Daddy colt made a quick impression.

"Even as a foal, he was awesome-looking and very intelligent," said John Gunther. "He was on the aggressive side and energetic. On the farm, he acted like he was the king. When he was in the field with the others he would give you that look like he had the sense he was the boss. He was a standout."

Tanya remembered him as being dominant among his classmates, "a big colt that filled your eye with his strength and power.

He looked more like a 2-year-old when he was a yearling. He made it readily apparent that you wouldn't want to challenge him, and that he was only humoring his handlers by allowing them to think that we were in charge."

One day when Justify was a weanling, he was one of the last of the group to be taken out to the paddock, and he wasn't happy about it.

"I'm a pretty fast walker," said Tanya, who was leading Justify out to the field. "This colt was just striding forward and with such purpose, covering so much ground. I can't recall handling a weanling doing that, where I couldn't keep up with him. It left an indelible impression on me. Needless to say, when he became a yearling and got bigger and stronger, he was the first to go out."

TO SELL OR
NOT TO SELL

ALTHOUGH THE GUNTHERS ENJOY OWNING RACEHORSES, AS commercial breeders their primary goal is selling them and turning a profit to keep the grass cut, the fences painted, the taxes paid, and their staff of 10 employed. As horse lovers, though, it is not easy for them to let go of their yearlings, whose births they have witnessed and who they've helped develop each step of the way. Going back to that fateful day Justify was born, Tanya and John Gunther felt the Scat Daddy colt was special, and father and daughter both had second thoughts about letting him go. But cash flow is cash flow, so Justify was entered in the 2016 Keeneland September sale of yearlings.

Ten months before that auction, Scat Daddy had died suddenly at Ashford Stud near Versailles, Kentucky, just outside Lexington in the heart of horse country. Ashford is owned by the worldwide Coolmore operation, the globe's largest breeder of Thoroughbreds. Founded by John Magnier, Coolmore had long dominated racing in Europe, and its deep pockets made it the likely winner of any bidding war for bloodstock at auctions worldwide. That is, at least until the Maktoum family, which rules Dubai (United Arab Emirates), got involved in the commercial Thoroughbred market in the 1980s, driving prices through the roof and delighting breeders as spirited bidding between the two huge entities became commonplace on the perceived best horses at sales.

Michael Tabor and Derrick Smith, two of Coolmore's partners, had bought an interest in Scat Daddy after his first two races. The colt, who was a son of Coolmore racehorse and champion Johannesburg, proved his talent by winning the grade 2 Sanford Stakes and the grade 1 Champagne Stakes in New York as a 2-year-old in 2006. He returned the following season to win the grade 2 Fountain of Youth Stakes and the grade 1 Florida Derby. In the Kentucky Derby, however, Scat Daddy was injured, ran unplaced, and was retired a month later.

Scat Daddy showed himself to be an excellent stallion as well, becoming the leading freshman sire of 2011, and four years later he had nine juvenile stakes winners in one year, setting a record. His death left a sizable hole in the Ashford Stud sire ranks, and at the 2016 Keeneland sale, Ashford was intent on purchasing as many of his yearling sons as possible in the hope that someday one or two of them would replace their sire in Coolmore's stallion complex.

"I thought if anyone was going to buy Justify, it would be Coolmore, because they were looking at and buying all the Scat Daddys, and our Scat Daddy was the best-looking one at the sale," said John Gunther.

At the Keeneland auction, some 5,000 yearlings go through the sale ring each September. In the days before they sell, they are inspected back at their consignors' barns. Top prospects can be pulled out of their stalls dozens of times a day, and possibly inspected by veterinarians who "scope," or inspect, their breathing passages by pushing a long instrument through the nose. It can be an extremely taxing experience for these young horses, and many do not handle it well. The Gunthers' Scat Daddy colt, though, seemed to relish all the attention without becoming nervous, a positive sign for how he would handle the rigors of the racetrack.

"He was confident, not stressed; rather just intrigued," noted Tanya Gunther of Justify. "It was like he was soaking it all up. You love to see that in a young horse because that demeanor and attitude bodes well for how they will handle the big race days you dream about them having down the road."

Justify received a good deal of attention and inspections. But in addition to visual examinations, each horse's leg X-rays are kept on file in a repository where veterinarians pore over them, looking for irregularities. One of the main gripes of sellers of bloodstock is that even the smallest imperfection causes the vets to recommend to buyers that they look elsewhere when spending their prodigious chunks of money on a young horse.

There are precious few secrets in the Thoroughbred business. It is a small universe to begin with, and news and rumors spread like wildfires on a dry summer day. The best-looking horses on the sale grounds will catch the attention of all the major buyers and their agents. And then it is up to the players to make their decisions about where to value a horse and what they can forgive of its physical flaws. John Gunther came to find out at some point just before the sale that Justify was suddenly off Coolmore's radar, and he knew something was up.

It turns out that a handful of vets flunked the Scat Daddy yearling because of a tiny OCD lesion they found on his X-rays. The common developmental imperfection in one of his joints was enough to turn many of the big buyers off him, but the roster of stakes winners overflows with horses who possessed less-than-perfect vet scores.

"It was just a tiny, minor thing, nothing," stated John Gunther. "We had done surgery on him and fixed it. But once I saw that Coolmore was off the horse, I knew that the veterinarians were flunking him. But I knew what we had there, and I wasn't about to give him away."

The consignor of every horse who goes through the sale ring puts a reserve price on them before bidding begins. If the bids don't reach the reserve number, the horse is deemed not sold and remains the property of his or her original owner.

John Gunther decided to make sure he didn't have seller's remorse and put a high reserve of $499,000 on the colt, thinking that for sure, given the vets' opinions, he would retain the Scat Daddy colt and eventually race him under the Glennwood banner. Which is exactly what he wanted to do deep down from the day the colt was born.

Divided emotionally on selling the horse anyway, the Gunthers may have found some odd relief in knowing their colt was considered flawed. Somebody was going to have to really love him at half a million dollars. The Gunthers already did and would be happy enough to bring him back home.

The Great Recession affected a vast array of businesses, the Thoroughbred industry squarely among them. Although most of the major stallion farms around the Bluegrass Region of Kentucky, the capital of the American Thoroughbred business, are long-established operations that have been run by generations of a single family, there are many small players in the business of raising and selling horses as well. For those people, selling a yearling for $50,000 could mean the difference between sending a child to college or not; or simply paying the monthly bills. While such transactions don't make the headlines of newspapers or industry publications, they are crucial for survival at the middle and lower ends of the horse industry.

The market for lesser horses took the biggest hit in the aftermath of the recession. While the wealthy players at the top of the market kept spending, albeit in curtailed amounts, the bottom of the market dropped off the table. Banks that had lent money to horse farmers based on the value of their equine stock saw those valuations cut in half virtually overnight and began calling in their paper. "For Sale" signs sprung up on every rural back lane in the region, and the Thoroughbred industry got downsized virtually overnight.

Even those larger farms with wealthy owners and firm financing in tow saw the need to cut costs wherever possible. Advertising dollars dried up and a long-standing industry publication, the venerable *Thoroughbred Times*, went out of business. Americans found themselves with less discretionary capital to spend, and thus handle—the money spent by gamblers on horse races that mostly goes to fund the purse money available to horse owners—also dove. Stallion owners made modest cuts to the fees they charged breeders to send their mares to be bred. And the amount of money buyers spent to buy bloodstock dove by nearly 50 percent.

Nevertheless, the market for top lots—the cream of the crop—remained relatively strong, even though the economic underpinnings of the Thoroughbred world stayed as risky as ever. With an annual foal crop of about 22,000 horses, only about 2 percent of those become winners of graded stakes races, the type of races that most increase the value of fillies and mares when they go on to second careers as broodmares; and make potential stallions out of colts. Considering the money needed to buy top prospects at yearling and 2-year-old sales, the financial risks inherent in the sport make it a zero-sum investment for participants. On average, they stand to lose half or two-thirds of their money.

Thus, to spread risk while also trying to buy more horses in the hope of getting one or two really good ones who defray the costs of the majority who don't pan out, even major players began entering into partnerships with one another coming out of the recession. WinStar Farm is one such entity. For a couple of years before Justify came along, WinStar formed a partnership with China Horse Club to buy yearlings together. Also joining that union was SF Bloodstock. Each of the three entities is well-funded and the hope is to spread the net wide enough so as to be able to buy more stock and increase the odds of finding those elite horses who will pay dividends on the racetrack and in their breeding careers.

A team of bloodstock advisors from each of those three entities comb the yearling sales for such prospects, and certainly the Keeneland September sale is the Woodstock of Thoroughbred auctions. Every prominent trainer and owner and bloodstock agent moves over the Keeneland grounds trying to get to as many of the 5,000 yearlings on offer as possible, certainly to all of the prime lots that sell in the auction's first few days.

David Hanley had for years been a successful trainer in Ireland, with numerous stakes winners to his credit including grade 1 winner Golden Apples and champion filly sprinter Lidanna. He had also been instrumental in buying top horses such as Chief Seattle, Forest Secrets, and WinStar Farm's second Belmont Stakes winner, Creator. Hanley serves as general manager of WinStar, and along with WinStar's president Elliott Walden, himself a former trainer as well, stalks the sale grounds searching for potential purchases for the organization.

A limited number of the sale's top prospects, based on physical inspections at farms in the months before the sale and on pedigree, are assigned to Book 1 at the Keeneland September sale. For Book 1, Hanley and Walden split up the horses between them and get around to inspect each one. They then talk over the horses who make their "short lists," and go look at the finalists together. Eventually they present a final roster of prospects to their partners China Horse Club and SF Bloodstock, who in 2016 had each sent their own bloodstock experts to the sale to examine the horses. China Horse Club and SF Bloodstock representatives then looked at the WinStar list, and either agreed to partner on the horses if WinStar bought them or decided against doing so on each individual on WinStar's list.

Hanley was particularly strong in his recommendation of Glennwood's Scat Daddy colt, and was joined in his assessment by Michael Wallace, who advised China Horse Club; and the SF Bloodstock team of Tom Ryan and Henry Field.

"Myself and Henry Field inspected all the horses we bid on with WinStar and China Horse Club," said SF's bloodstock head Tom Ryan. "We both loved Justify. There was unanimity among all the owners that we should do our best to buy him, and it was an easy decision to try."

"All three of the partnership entities liked that horse," said Hanley. "It was a positive 'Let's go buy him.' We had heard about the horse being failed by other vets, but we use two veterinarians to examine the horses, and both were fine with the horse. There was never a question about him having an issue. He had undergone a surgery, but he was fine. He passed our vets' inspection and they gave us the go-ahead to try and buy him."

Ryan agreed after checking with his vet, Dr. Mike Hore. "We were unconcerned about his X-rays," Ryan stated. "We have enormous confidence in our vet, who passed him, and we saw an opportunity because others may fail or discount the horse."

That would have been a relief to Hanley, who was adamant that WinStar should do everything it could to secure the colt.

"We like to focus on horses that are bred to go two turns [longer distances], and look like they have the physical build to go two turns," said Hanley. "When Justify was brought out of the barn and put in front of you, he had that beautiful shape to him with a lot of leg and stretch. For a big horse, he had that length to his hip and hind leg, and a lot of muscle so that he didn't look like a big, backward horse. He looked like he would have some speed. He moved well and was easy to like. It was a question of him filling out into his frame, but he was obviously a very nice horse.

"When you see the pictures of him as a yearling, he had that big skeletal structure, a big frame. Sometimes those big horses are slow and don't have the movement. This horse carried himself lightly on his feet. He had no drag and wasn't weak in any way. In hindsight, everybody says they loved him. I know I was a big part in us buying the horse. With his size and strength and the way he moved, I felt he was very special, and I thought, 'Man, we have to buy this horse.' Elliott got on board, and the other partners were 100 percent game as well."

In addition to the physical specimen and how a horse moves, evaluators also talk about intangibles that can radiate out from a potential racehorse. There is "the look of eagles" in a horse's eye, or a sense of calm that reflects intelligence. Hanley was just as certain in these aspects as he was about the muscles and bone structure he was studying.

"Obviously, there's a lot to the vibe you get off a horse and their personality, and this horse had a huge presence," he noted. "When he moved, it was like a big, clumsy child moving like Michael Jordan. Just the way he walked and got across the ground, his action and balance. Every picture you see of him, he's always perfectly square, perfectly balanced without anybody having to set him up. His presence is quite incredible. He's a unique horse."

Justify entered the Keeneland sale ring as Hip #50 in the prestigious Book 1 of the sale. Breeder John Gunther watched intently as the bidding escalated, hoping his reserve of $499,000 was high enough to dissuade potential buyers. Cash flow may be key to running his Glennwood Farm, but Gunther, remembering back to the day that Justify was foaled and his and Tanya's first thoughts about the special circumstances surrounding his arrival, was hoping to keep this colt. Hanley, though, was equally as passionate about the chestnut beauty in the sale ring. The bidding progressed steadily, as several entities were "in" on the horse. One was New York businessman Robert LaPenta, who had won many prestigious races, including the Belmont Stakes (he would win a second Belmont Stakes less than a year later). LaPenta offered $450,000 for the Scat Daddy colt but dropped out of play when the bidding blew past that amount.

At that point, WinStar was bidding against the $499,000 reserve instead of against other potential buyers. Walden made a final bid of $500,000. When the hammer fell, the Scat Daddy colt had been sold to WinStar, China Horse Club, and SF Bloodstock for half a million dollars.

"You need some luck and some good judgment; maybe a lot of luck and less good judgment," Hanley noted. "We've been doing this for a while and we got lucky. But he was a good horse, too, and met a lot of the criteria that we look for. He's a beautiful horse."

Gunther didn't exactly act like a man who had just received $500,000 for a yearling he bred on a $30,000 stud fee, a huge win for any breeder. He hated to see the horse leave. In fact, he sought to make a deal with WinStar to remain in for a share of the colt, but the percentages had already been determined by WinStar and its two partners, and there was nothing left over to offer to the breeder.

"It was depressing," Gunther said.

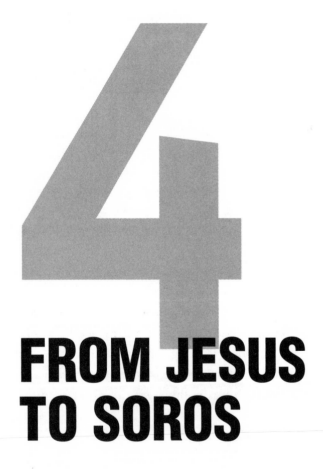

FROM JESUS TO SOROS

IN THIS AGE OF GLOBALIZATION, MERGERS, AND ACQUISITIONS, in which companies are bought and sold to the point where most people don't know who owns what—or even what country owns what—Justify offers a perfect reflection of the times. The three groups that shared his purchase price at the Keeneland sale have roots in Australia, Ireland, China, Hungary, and the American Midwest. Then, after his first race, one of his owners sold its rights to Justify's racing career; the other two sold off a slice of theirs; two new groups came in to buy those pieces of his racing career; and all three original owners ultimately sold the colt's breeding rights to an entirely different operation. It was almost as if Justify was being day-traded throughout his first three years.

If Seabiscuit's story mirrored the Great Depression and how a great horse could change lives, Justify's represents the complicated web that comes with the age of corporate capitalism in the modern world.

WinStar Farm took the lead role in buying Justify from John Gunther's Glennwood Farm at the Keeneland September sale, maintaining a 60 percent share in the horse. China Horse Club ponied up for 25 percent (known as owning a "leg" in the horse business, since one leg makes up 25 percent of the horse's four legs), and SF Bloodstock held the remaining 15 percent. Those three entities had been in partnership on certain bloodstock for a couple of years before the deal for Justify, at a 50/25/25 split before SF decided in 2016 to reduce its position in the partnership horses from 25 percent to 15 percent.

If politics make strange bedfellows, so too do horse partnerships. WinStar, China Horse Club, and SF Bloodstock couldn't be more different in their origins, but when business beckons that can potentially make money for partners long-term while saving in the short term, pen gets put to paper.

The story of WinStar Farm begins far from the 3,000 lush acres that today comprise the farm along Pisgah Pike in beautiful Woodford County outside Lexington, Kentucky. On April 29, 1975, at the now-defunct Ak-Sar-Ben (Nebraska spelled backward) racetrack, Kenny Troutt, who owned a few horses who probably couldn't outrun him; and Bill Casner, who trained a couple of horses whose names nobody would remember, put in claim slips for the same horse on the track's opening day.

In claiming races, which are usually for stock that has not exhibited overwhelming talent, each horse is for sale for a pre-determined amount listed in the conditions of the race. Anyone interested in buying, or claiming, a horse drops a slip in a box in the racing office no later than 20 minutes before post time. They become the owners of the horse after that race. If two or more parties put in claim slips on the same horse, a "shake" is held after the race, so named for the pills that are put in a bottle and then shaken before one is pulled out to determine the winner of the claim.

Troutt and Casner both had their eye on Great Bear Lake, a son of Gallant Man available that day for $6,250. Casner, a native Texan, spent his boyhood summers riding horses at a cousin's ranch in Central Texas, and at 12 made his first bet at Sunland Park. A year later he was breaking and galloping horses at the track. He began working around the Midwest, and eventually took a job on the starting gate at Ak-Sar-Ben, finding time to train a few horses on the side. By 1974 he was training full time, on a circuit from Louisiana up through Arkansas and into Chicago.

Troutt grew up in Mt. Vernon, Illinois, and had an uncle who raced horses at Cahokia Downs and Fairmont Park. Troutt took an immediate liking to the racing game, and as a senior in college got in the sport by buying his first horse for $1,500. Troutt moved to Nebraska and started a breeding farm and training center.

"Bill won the shake for Great Bear Lake," remembered Troutt. "I claimed a horse in a similar class, and we competed against each other. I saw that he had success with that horse and did a good job with him. So when I'd run into Bill, we'd talk and eventually became friends."

Troutt gave Casner his horses to train, and the two began claiming inexpensive stock together. When Troutt started a family, he decided to give up the horse game to settle down to a more stable lifestyle.

In fact, Troutt and Casner, born two months apart in 1948, both got out of the horse business and moved, separately, to Texas. Casner became a successful Snap-On Tools franchise operator and also invested in the oil business with Troutt, an enterprise that boomed...for a while. When it busted, Troutt moved on to establish Excel Communications with financial backing from Casner. In 1988 Troutt was the sole employee of the company, and eventually figured out he could make money reselling long-distance phone service on other companies' networks.

By 1995 Excel was doing $1 billion of business a year and was the fourth-largest long-distance company in the country. It was the youngest company ever to go public on the New York Stock

Exchange, and Troutt and Casner owned 100 percent of it when it did. In 1998 they sold Excel to Teleglobe for $3.5 billion.

"During that time the two of us would get together and talk about horses like old fraternity brothers, telling the same stories over and over," Troutt said. "In the back of our minds, we said if we ever got back in we wanted to do it at the high end."

Casner met Art Preston, who, with his brothers J.R. and Jack, had a successful racing stable and farm called Prestonwood. Casner and Art Preston bought some horses under the name Full Circle Racing, and soon Troutt and Casner were traveling with the Preston brothers to big races, including to New York to watch the Prestons' Victory Gallop, trained by Elliott Walden, win the 1998 Belmont Stakes and 1999 Whitney Stakes. In late 1999, Troutt and Casner approached the Prestons about buying Prestonwood Farm.

Troutt and Casner closed on Prestonwood's 400 acres in early 2000, buying the land, broodmare band, and most of the stallion interests. They quickly acquired an additional 600 acres and set about building new barns, offices, and constructing a picturesque pond visible from Pisgah Pike, a beautiful country lane that stretches about five miles with 18th century churches bookending it. Albert "Happy" Chandler, the second commissioner of baseball, is buried next to the church on the Versailles Road side of Pisgah Pike.

You can mark up all the business plans you want for the horse industry, but you still have to be lucky to succeed. Casner noted that both he and Troutt considered the newly renamed WinStar Farm to be their primary business when they started it. "We've spent a tremendous amount of time thinking about it and working on it," he said. "It's a passion and a tremendous challenge, because at the high end maybe 5 percent of the people in [the horse business] make money."

Their good luck came in the form of two of the stallions they inherited from Prestonwood. Victory Gallop's first crop to race made better than $900,000, making him the second-best first-crop sire in North America. But it was Distorted Humor who really put WinStar on the map. A grade 2 winner who was trained by Walden for the latter part of his career, Distorted Humor became a sensation at stud. His New York–bred son Funny Cide rose from oblivion to win the 2003 Kentucky Derby and Preakness Stakes, becoming a national sensation. By 2005 Distorted Humor was the #2 sire in North America and a perennial Top 10 sire after that, becoming North America's leading sire by progeny earnings in 2011, the year before his son Drosselmeyer won the Belmont for WinStar.

Elliott Walden in the early 2000s became the private trainer for WinStar, training exclusively for Troutt and Casner. After a few years, Walden retired from the track and was brought into WinStar as vice president and racing manager. He has since risen to president.

WinStar has steadily grown its stallion population and is home to more than two dozen stud horses today. It built a beautiful new stallion complex in 2013 that looks more like a five-star hotel and has become a major player at the top of the business alongside far more established Thoroughbred operations such as Three Chimneys Farm, Lane's End Farm, and Claiborne Farm. Its racing stable won the 2011 Kentucky Derby with Super Saver and the Belmont with not only Drosselmeyer, but also Creator (2016).

"Sometimes Bill [Casner] and I take a breath and look at each other and say what we're doing is living a dream," Troutt said after their first Belmont Stakes victory. "Back in Nebraska, we'd dream about going to Saratoga sometime just to see a race. This is a great thrill. We have a little joke between us: 'We're a long ways from Nebraska.'"

WinStar has given back through various charitable donations through the years. It funds the Race for Education, a national scholarship program that provides educational opportunities to children of racetrack and farm workers. In 2002, Troutt became a born-again Christian and has helped fund the Racetrack Chaplaincy program. He created the annual White Horse Award that recognizes heroic service. Walden is also a devout Christian. Justify was named for a Biblical reference from Romans 9 and 10, which talks about being justified by faith.

The Troutt-Casner partnership was dissolved in 2010 when Troutt bought out his partner's interest in WinStar, which had already begun looking to form strategic partnerships in order to be able to continue buying premier bloodstock. That led to its relationship with SF Bloodstock.

The partnership of WinStar and SF Bloodstock got off to a good start in 2008 when SF invested in a WinStar-bred yearling named Super Saver, the eventual Derby winner. It was an auspicious entry into the Thoroughbred business for SF Bloodstock, whose principals tend to be largely media-shy.

SF Bloodstock is known in the Thoroughbred industry as a "trader," that is, a group that is willing to buy and sell stock at what it deems is the right price, with far less interest in actually racing horses, although today it is now planning a bit more racing than it has engaged in over its first decade. SF has invested heavily in buying a quality broodmare band—several, actually—to service its extensive stallion interests in the United States, Europe, and Australia, where it co-owns Newgate Farm and interests in Newgate's stallion roster. In the past couple of years alone SF Bloodstock has bought, for six- and seven-figure sums, graded stakes winners such as Cathryn Sophia, Illuminant,

Pricedtoperfection, Paola Queen, Unbridled Belle, Gold Canyon, and My Conquestadory for its broodmare ranks. In Europe, SF Bloodstock has acquired Starlight Dreams, the dam of grade 1 winner Mastercraftsman; and Mrs Marsh, the dam of grade 1 winner Canford Cliffs.

It is also not unusual for SF to sell stock shortly after purchasing it or purchasing mares in foal and selling the resulting weanlings the following year.

According to various industry participants, SF Bloodstock was formed by Australian Gavin Murphy, who for 20 years has worked for Soros Fund Management. Soros Fund Management was established in 1970 by Hungarian expatriate George Soros, who is well known in financial and political circles if not in the horse racing world. Under Soros' direction, his fund for 40 years realized average annual returns of 20 percent, making him one of the world's wealthiest people with a worth of some $30 billion. Soros has become even more famous as a lightning rod for his political contributions to liberal causes in the United States, and was said to have contributed at least $7 million to Hillary Clinton's failed 2016 presidential campaign.

Murphy, whose tenure at Soros Fund Management represents an unusually long stint for that operation, is listed as "Director, Tax" of the organization. Murphy wanted to retire from Soros' employ to engage full time in his passion of working in the horse business. Soros, though, didn't want his valued executive to depart, and asked Murphy to explain the horse business to him, especially the potential of making money in it. The two men worked out a deal. Murphy, who is loyal to the now-88-year-old Soros, agreed to stay on with the firm, while Soros helped establish and bankroll SF Bloodstock, which has grown from a relatively small operation to a global Thoroughbred bloodstock powerhouse managed by Murphy.

SF Bloodstock owns more than 100 broodmares in the U.S. alone, which are employed in the service of its vast stallion interests. Not surprisingly, SF is run similarly to a financial fund, with an eye always to the bottom line. And it has successfully made money since its inception. The horses bred by SF Bloodstock are offered, mainly at yearling sales, through a variety of outside consignors, as SF has not established its own consignment presence.

Tom Ryan, a graduate of the prestigious Irish National Stud program that teaches horsemanship to natives of Ireland, is the most visible member of the SF team. Based in Lexington, Kentucky, Ryan heads the group's bloodstock division, which was particularly active buying yearlings out of the 2018 Keeneland September sale. Ryan has worked in the horse industry in Australia, Japan, and the U.S., forming his own Cherokee Equine in 2007 before meeting Murphy and joining SF Bloodstock.

Ryan also helped assemble a management team for the third leg of Justify's original ownership tripod, China Horse Club. That startup organization joined up in 2015 with WinStar and SF Bloodstock to buy yearlings and 2-year-olds on a three-year deal that has since expired. But it was under that arrangement that the trio purchased Justify, as well as Audible, a horse who also became a multiple graded stakes winner, a grade 1 winner, and ran against Justify in the Kentucky Derby, finishing third.

Founded in 2013 by its CEO Teo Ah King, China Horse Club (CHC) hopes to persuade the Chinese government to approve gambling on horse racing in Mainland China. Marketed to wealthy Chinese with limited outlets in which to spend their money, CHC in no time filled its initial membership goal of 300 investors who bought in at $1 million (U.S.) apiece. CHC has used that capital to purchase top Thoroughbred stock and develop leisure properties, including a new racetrack on the Caribbean island of St. Lucia. It is selling a lifestyle of glamour that includes participation in horse racing.

Teo is a construction executive whose interest in racing was kindled when he served as contractor for the Meydan racetrack in the United Arab Emirates, home to the Dubai World Cup, the world's richest Thoroughbred race. He seeks to raise interest in the sport on the Mainland to the extent where the government, which has not given any indication it approves of the goal, would be moved toward approving the operation of racetracks as well as legalizing gambling.

"This is a country ruled by popular support," Teo told *BloodHorse* magazine in 2016. "I think when the momentum catches up and millions are watching horse racing, by sheer force a lot of things will happen and the government will do something drastic [approve wagering]."

CHC hosted a race day in the Inner Mongolian province of Ordos in 2016 that drew 26,000, with more than a million other Chinese participating in the live streaming of the races. UAE interests have staged three race meetings in Sichuan Province, importing the horses from Dubai. Racing has long thrived in Hong Kong, and the Hong Kong Jockey Club has built a training center north of Hong Kong that could be converted to a racetrack.

While pushing for an expansion of racing in China, CHC has enjoyed early success in established jurisdictions. In 2017, CHC scored a huge win in the U.S. when 3-year-old filly Abel Tasman, trained by Bob Baffert, won the Kentucky Oaks. She has gone right on winning for CHC and co-owner Clearsky Farms, taking additional grade 1 events the Acorn Stakes and Coaching Club American Oaks in 2017 and scoring in the Ogden Phipps Stakes and Personal Ensign Stakes in 2018. She won more than $2.7 million, and in January of 2018 was sold at auction to Coolmore for $5 million as a broodmare prospect.

CHC also co-owns Saratoga grade 2 winner Good Samaritan, and co-owned multiple European grade 1 winner Australia. Such high-profile victories, while fueling the passion of CHC's members and furthering that brand, also serves as a model for growing horse racing in China and pushing the government toward support.

Meanwhile, CHC is constructing a racetrack with stabling for 1,000 horses on St. Lucia as part of a complex that is slated to include residences and hotels. Called "Pearl of the Caribbean," the development seems another avenue to offer wealthy Chinese investment opportunities off the Mainland, purportedly by offering dual citizenship. The racetrack was scheduled to open in February of 2019. A measure of CHC's pull was seen at Churchill Downs when Justify ran in the 2018 Kentucky Derby. Teo had in tow Allen Chastanet, the prime minister of St. Lucia. WinStar's Walden has attended the last two editions of the China Equine Cultural Festival on the Mainland.

"Racing can just explode here one day into like it is in Europe or Australia or in the United States," Walden told *BloodHorse*. "I love coming here, and maybe one day we can bring a WinStar-bred to win a race."

As Justify left the Keeneland sale grounds for the short van ride to WinStar Farm, he couldn't have possibly known the international scope and various tentacles of his ownership group. But he certainly had become, on a bid of $500,000, a horse for the modern era.

5
EARLY LESSONS AT THE FARM

RICHARD BUDGE'S OFFICE WAS A SMALL CABIN SET ON A RISE over the WinStar Farm training track. From his perch Budge could oversee the progress of young horses as they took their first spins around the synthetic surface, engineered to stay dry and usable even in extreme bouts of rain or cold. WinStar's more advanced youngsters were shipped over to Budge's division in December of their yearling season, with the next group arriving roughly a month after they became 2-year-olds. (Thoroughbreds are generally born between January and June, but regardless of their actual foaling dates, all become a year older each January 1.)

WinStar had become one of the premier training facilities in the U.S. for Thoroughbreds. It is open to outside horses from other owners who require rest and rehabilitation due to soreness, injury, or post-surgical recovery. Recent grade 1 winners such as Little Mike, Bal a Bali, and Honor Code have all spent time at WinStar rehabbing in between races. In addition, Budge oversaw the early lessons for WinStar's yearlings and 2-year-olds before they were shipped to various racetrack trainers across the country.

Budge, who announced after Justify's Triple Crown season that he was leaving WinStar, was uniquely qualified for his work. A native of England, he worked as an assistant training steeplechase horses there, and then assisted trainer Jonathan Pease with Thoroughbreds in France. He did a four-year stint in Brazil training yearlings and 2-year-olds for the respected Rio Claro Thoroughbreds before coming to the U.S. and serving as an assistant to Steve DiMauro Sr. Budge then became private trainer for Art Preston in Texas, where he conditioned Texas champion Special Moments.

In the Lone Star State, Bill Casner and Kenny Troutt had a few horses in a syndicate with Preston, and Budge took them up on an offer to come to WinStar in 2002 to become the farm trainer there. At the time, WinStar was training its horses at the HighPointe Training Center near La Grange, Kentucky. The program had already graduated star runners such as Any Given Saturday, Colonel John, Bluegrass Cat, and Drosselmeyer.

"We felt we wanted the entire operation closer to home, so in 2009 we decided to build a training center here at the farm," explained Elliott Walden. "We wanted the opportunity to have a commercial arm to add to our stallion side."

WinStar could not have asked for better results once its training program moved to the farm and opened in 2010. WinStar-owned Super Saver won that year's Kentucky Derby and Drosselmeyer the Belmont Stakes. As for outside horses, Uncle Mo was sent to WinStar after he became ill and failed to make the 2011 Derby. After spending two months at WinStar, he returned to win a grade 2 stakes, becoming a prominent advertisement for the farm's rehab side.

"We do layups and training for clients as well as WinStar horses, and the facility has all the tools for post-surgery horses," Budge noted before Justify won the Triple Crown. "We can do stall rest, hand-walking, paddock turnout, Aquatred [swimming], spa, hyperbaric chamber, and then the racetrack, where we can get published workouts and have a certified gate crew from Keeneland. Horses don't have to move from one facility to another."

Added Walden, "The big thing is treating each horse individually. Time is money, and when you're rehabbing a horse, it can get lost on a farm and lose condition, and then it takes a while to get them back to where you can train them. Here, even though a horse gets turned out, we can swim them, put them in a cold-water spa or a hyperbaric chamber. So when they're ready to start back training, they're already in shape and you don't increase the time needed away from the racetrack."

Before WinStar's young horses reached Budge's tutelage, they'd already gone through a highly delineated program designed to get them accustomed to their upcoming careers.

After Justify was taken to WinStar directly from the Keeneland sale grounds in September of 2016, he was given two weeks in a paddock buddied up with another yearling. The two weeks allow the young horses to relax after the rigors of the sale, and having a friend in the small paddock generally makes them easier to manage. After that initial two weeks, the yearlings are sent across Pisgah Pike to the former Hopewell Farm, which was purchased by WinStar a couple of years before Justify's arrival, to be broken.

The breaking process consists of getting young horses used to things that are taken for granted once they become racehorses. Here, they are saddled for the first time. They have someone lie on their backs, getting them used to feeling that weight. They are worked on long lines (lunge lines), or ropes, trotting around in circles in an indoor arena.

The husband-and-wife team of Toby and Heather Richard do the breaking of the WinStar babies. They joined the WinStar staff in 2016 with plenty of experience under their belt buckles. Toby grew up in Cajun Country in Louisiana riding and breaking horses, then hit the road for two decades working for top trainers such as Bill Mott, Steve Asmussen, and Nick Zito. Heather broke horses in her native Florida before working as an exercise rider and assistant trainer for Dale Romans, Wayne Lukas, and Todd Pletcher.

"We've fallen in love working with the babies here," Heather said. "They're so impressionable and want to learn. You show them A to B and they pick it up so quickly. It's fun to watch their personalities from Day One and see them grow."

The Richards break in the vicinity of 70 horses a year at WinStar, yet neither had any trouble remembering their Scat Daddy pupil from the autumn of 2016.

"A lot of the horses here are really special, but he stood out as a tall, good-minded horse," said Heather. "He was confident and smart; forward and interested; everything you could ask for in a good horse. When we hear people compliment him as a 'good-minded horse,' we know that we played a part in that and did our job."

Added Toby, "Justify had a good personality; he was an easy-going colt. I rode him inside the barn a couple of days and then out in the round pen, and saddle-broke him. Drove him with long lines in the round pen and then rode him in the arena. We give them a few challenges to overcome, like stepping over logs and having horses come at one another, and he came through it with the greatest of ease."

The yearlings are also taken on trail rides through the farm and are ridden on uphill gallops as well as galloped on the training track. They are aligned on the track with two horses in front and one behind, getting them used to the type of situation they'll face when their racing days begin. Importantly, the Richards also teach their charges how to enter and stand in the starting gate. The starting gate can be a claustrophobic and intimidating place for a robust Thoroughbred, and it is crucial that they be rewarded and gotten accustomed to the gate being a safe place for them. By the time the Richards passed their pupils off to Budge at the training barn, the horses will have done everything but breeze, which is a full-speed workout.

Justify arrived with the second group of yearlings who were sent to the training barn on December 21, 2016.

"He wouldn't have been one we'd identify as a potential early-in-the-year 2-year-old to race five furlongs at Saratoga," noted WinStar's David Hanley. "We always thought he would be more of a later 2-year-old that could make the races toward the end of that year."

Three months after he arrived at the training division, Justify was sent out with a group of his peers for his first breeze, a quarter-mile sprint along the training track. On that March 22, 2017, day, three former trainers—Budge, Hanley, and Walden—assembled at the small cabin overlooking the track. Incredibly, three of the young WinStar 2-year-olds they were there to watch would make it to the starting gate of the Kentucky Derby less than 14 months later.

The horses breezed in pairs going along the uphill course, including the imposing chestnut colt with a prominent blaze who flashed past the assembled, making an immediate impression.

"My mouth was wide-open. His stride was so long and so impressive and effortless," noted Budge. "It was like, 'What did I just see?' We all looked at each other and knew the horse was really good. So when the rider came back, we asked him very nonchalantly what he thought. He gave the horse a pat and said, 'He's unbelievable. Like California Chrome.'"

California Chrome had won the 2014 Kentucky Derby and Preakness.

"What is so impressive to me is that he stood out above the best horses we had back then, even though he was an immature colt who was still growing," Budge said. "You look at each group that comes in and you pick out five or so that you feel are the cream of the crop. And he stood out against the best of them. It is very gratifying that we saw that early on."

Said Walden, "The other horses were working really hard and he was just floating along the top, and he looked special at that point."

Among the horses against whom Justify stood out were Audible, who would become a grade 1 winner; Noble Indy, who would contest the Derby and Belmont Stakes against Justify the following year; and Quip, who would compete in the Preakness Stakes.

Justify began growing into his frame as a 2-year-old early in 2017, presenting a conundrum for the WinStar training staff.

"When these young horses get their growth spurt, they can find it hard to gain weight," noted Hanley. "Justify has such a big frame and was growing at such a rate that we wanted to give him a chance to catch up. You always wonder whether one like him is going to get too big."

Budge and the WinStar brass were no doubt excited about what they were seeing from Justify in his early breezes, but they needed to balance their enthusiasm against the notion that giving the colt too much to do too soon could be detrimental to his development.

"He was a growing colt with such a big, long stride and big action to him that it was obvious he would improve with time and blossom later in the year, or even early the following year," said Budge. "Anytime you have a horse showing you that much talent and looking more like a 3-year-old than a 2-year-old, you give them the time to strengthen and mature."

When Justify sustained a minor injury, it made the decision easier to give him a break and some paddock turnout. Most horsemen are in no huge rush to start their 2-year-olds in races. At major racetracks, races for juveniles are not written until April, and even that is considered too early for those horsemen with expensive stock. Early summer is when many of the promising 2-year-olds are unleashed. It usually takes a couple of months for horses to acclimate to the racetrack, and so even the most forward of the WinStar 2-year-olds are not shipped to their racetrack trainers until around the middle of May. Justify, however, was not among that group. While some of his paddock and training track buddies were flown to their racetrack trainers around the country right after Kentucky Derby week, Justify in mid-May was sent on a much shorter journey.

Having strained a hock, Justify's exercise was cut back for several weeks during which he was only walked, then was turned out in a small paddock for a month, getting a complete break from training. When he returned to the training division, Budge noted an extreme difference in the Scat Daddy colt.

"It's amazing how much they grow and gather strength during that time," he noted. "When we brought him back, Justify had turned into a beast."

Justify had already gone through the rudimentary steps in his training before his mini-vacation. He'd learned about the starting gate and had already begun breezing. Also working in his favor was that mental aspect of his constitution that cannot be overemphasized.

"He is just a brilliant, intelligent horse," said John Gunther. "To me, he's almost human. A very cool individual. Nothing ever bothered him."

Over the course of that summer, Justify was sent out at WinStar for a series of quarter-mile and three-eighths-mile breezes. While Justify could have been sent to trainer Bob Baffert in California in late summer, WinStar made the decision to give him more seasoning close to home. The previous year, WinStar had begun sending many of its 2-year-olds to Keeneland just a couple of miles from the farm. There, trainer Rudolphe Bisset got them acclimated to racetrack life and put the topping on their training.

On August 23, 2017, Justify was vanned to Keeneland.

"Since the training track at WinStar is a synthetic surface, the transition to Keeneland gets them used to a dirt surface," said Budge. "They also get to see the grandstand and experience more horses out on the track with them. We filled Rudolphe in on what we thought of Justify; the kind of horse he was to gallop and breeze, and he put the finishing touches on him and did well with him."

After spending nearly two months at Keeneland, Justify on November 8, 2017, was finally flown to California and the stable of Bob Baffert, leaving behind his teachers and trainers at WinStar, who would be left to monitor his continued progress anxiously from afar.

Asked if he'd given Baffert any information on Justify, Budge let out a laugh. "Oh, good Lord, no. You do treat horses like they're your children, and you're a little sad when they leave. We knew the kind of horse we thought he'd be, and you hope he pans out to be what you hope for."

6
CALIFORNIA
DREAMING

THE BREEDERS' CUP WORLD CHAMPIONSHIPS, A LOFTY TITLE given to a brace of races that were established in 1984 to give Thoroughbred racing another big day on the calendar and determine year-end champions in various divisions, in 2017 was held at Del Mar for the first time. The scenic seaside vacation town 20 minutes north of San Diego nestles between the Pacific Ocean and gentle inland hills, and the Del Mar racetrack, founded by Bing Crosby and a variety of other Hollywood luminaries in the 1930s as a summertime getaway from Los Angeles, is so close to the Pacific that its tagline is "Where the turf meets the surf."

Del Mar and another iconic Thoroughbred venue, Keeneland, were once thought to be too small to host the Breeders' Cup, which shuttled in its first decades largely among giant plants such as Santa Anita Park, Churchill Downs, and Belmont Park. But the event has seen a makeover in recent years and its board has shown an affinity toward "destination sites" that are more pleasing to sponsors, advertisers, and marketers. Breeders' Cup can make as much, and likely more, money drawing crowds of 30,000 who are willing to pay high-end prices for more amenities, as it can attracting 70,000 general-admission fans.

Everyone who is anyone in the industry attends the Breeders' Cup. Trainer Bob Baffert, stabled two hours north at Santa

Anita, is one of Del Mar's signature participants for its regular summer meeting that runs from late July to early September. For this Breeders' Cup, Baffert's headline horse is Arrogate, winner of the 2016 Breeders' Cup Classic, the richest of all the Breeders' Cup races, when he overcame a seemingly impossible lead established by the popular California Chrome and overtook that rival with 100 yards to go before a stunned grandstand at Santa Anita.

Arrogate, the 2016 3-year-old Horse of the Year on the strength of that victory and a record-smashing win in Saratoga's Travers Stakes two months before, had suddenly lost his form in the second half of 2017. After an impressive score in the January 2017 Pegasus World Cup, the world's richest race that year with a $16 million purse, and a thrilling come-from-behind win in the March Dubai World Cup, the second-richest race of that season, Arrogate had been going the wrong way, most recently before the Breeders' Cup faltering badly in the San Diego Handicap at Del Mar. Baffert, for all his skills, couldn't seem to unlock the reason behind Arrogate's form reversal, and it was weighing on him. No horseman enjoys seeing a superstar under his care suddenly lose his mojo, and owners begin to get edgy when they sense a horse is hurting his stud value with a series of underachieving performances.

So Baffert had plenty on his mind in the days leading up to the 2017 Breeders' Cup, and probably took little solace when Elliott Walden sidled up to him that week and told him WinStar Farm wanted to send Baffert a promising 2-year-old colt to train. WinStar owner Kenny Troutt, along with Walden and China Horse Club's bloodstock advisor Michael Wallace, had all agreed to send Baffert a couple of horses the previous year for the first time, and Baffert had done well, winning stakes races with American Anthem. Baffert would have known Walden well enough from Walden's training days, and the memory for Baffert wasn't pleasant.

In 1998, Baffert's second Kentucky Derby and Preakness winner in as many years, Real Quiet, was going for the Triple Crown in the Belmont Stakes (which at the time included a $5 million bonus if a horse won the Triple Crown) and opened a five-length lead at the head of the long Belmont stretch. Real Quiet, owned by Baffert's good friend Mike Pegram, looked home free. But Victory Gallop, a top flight and developing colt, came from seemingly nowhere and hit the wire together with Real Quiet. After an agonizing wait for the photo finish to be examined, Victory Gallop's number was put up on top of the toteboard. Victory Gallop's trainer? Elliott Walden.

WinStar races most all of its horses on the East Coast with trainers such as Bill Mott and Todd Pletcher. With its various partnerships established over the past few years, WinStar had upped its annual yearling purchases from 20 to 30, and that in part necessitated separating its youngsters to a greater extent and spreading them around. Certainly Baffert, who had won a Triple Crown less than three years earlier, was an attractive candidate for any owner looking to develop their horses for the classic races for 3-year-olds, and Walden, in that Breeders' Cup week, let Baffert know he'd elected to send WinStar's husky Scat Daddy colt to him.

"Well, you know, any horse makes sense for Bob, really," said Walden in explanation. "A lot of why we give horses to certain trainers is kind of a gut feel about each horse. As far as this horse goes, one of the important factors is we were behind the eight ball. He was going into training late, and although not every horse is going to run in the Triple Crown races, we do focus on them and you want to try and give them every opportunity. The weather in California is very consistent, so generally they won't miss any training due to weather, and all of those things were considerations.

"I also appreciate Bob's camaraderie and his communication skills, which is important to me, that we can communicate on a level where I know what's going on whether the horse is 50 miles down the road or 3,000 miles down the road. And Bob's been great that way.

"Plus, if you're going to send a horse to Bob, you want him in the first flight, and this looked like a very good horse, a very smart horse who handled everything well, and we tried to hire a very good trainer. Maybe the greatest of all time."

Arrogate indeed ran poorly once again trying to defend his title in the 2017 Breeders' Cup Classic and was retired after that race to stand stud at the farm of his owners, Juddmonte, in Lexington. Four days after the running of the Classic, in early November, Justify stepped off the jet that carried him from Kentucky to California and was vanned to Los Alamitos Race Course in the sleepy town of Cypress, 15 miles south of Los Angeles. Barn space and the number of stalls available at Santa Anita Park are limited, especially with the closing of Hollywood Park in 2014. Trainers who were fortunate enough to have a full contingent of horses had to scramble to find stall space for their overflow of stock, especially the 2-year-olds who shipped in over the second half of each year to begin their racetrack training.

Los Alamitos stepped in to fill the stabling void in Southern California. Traditionally a Quarter Horse track, Los Alamitos ran some Thoroughbred races as well. Quarter Horses run sprints, or shorter races, and Los Alamitos, after deciding to pick up some of the racing dates formerly run at Hollywood Park, expanded its racetrack layout to more easily accommodate longer contests. It also offered its stalls to Thoroughbred trainers in need. Baffert's operation at Santa Anita Park can hold roughly 100 horses, and when the rookies ship in, those 2-year-olds get their first taste of the racetrack at Los Alamitos, where Baffert will keep about 75 2-year-olds.

When Justify alighted from the van that brought him to Los Alamitos from the airport, he was greeted by Mike Marlow, Baffert's assistant in charge of the string at "Los Al," as it is affectionately called. Marlow, a former Quarter Horse jockey back in his native Illinois, had been an assistant to Wayne Lukas for 13 years before going out on his own in 2002. Marlow carved out an existence for seven years as a head trainer, but with mostly cheap horses running for low purse money, the economics of the game eventually overtook him. Lukas had given Marlow a glowing recommendation when Baffert asked about him, and Marlow went to work for Baffert at the beginning of 2010. He gets the independence of running Baffert's division at Los Al along with the benefit of handling good horses, and he surely knows a really good one when he sees it.

"At the time Justify got off the van, he was just another big, good-looking horse that we get here," said Marlow. "It's kind of funny—we have one full barn and then one side of two other barns here, and we put them in stalls as we get them. How the dominoes fell, Justify ended up in our third barn in the very last stall. Not that it's a bad spot, but of the 70 to 75 2-year-olds we had, he was one of the last to come in. Very few come that late, and the ones that do usually have had setbacks earlier in the year."

Marlow's job is to take the 2-year-olds, who have shipped in from around the country, and get them acclimated to Baffert's training program. Although the horses have already breezed at their previous homes, Marlow builds them up again in a progression that starts with workouts of three-eighths of a mile and moves along to longer distances. Justify handled his first three-eighths breeze with aplomb, and Marlow remembers him being impressive-looking, but added, "A lot of them are impressive going three-eighths. When we get them up to five-eighths of a mile, that usually separates them, and he worked in :59 and change dragging the rider out of the saddle. That's your first pretty good indication that they're on the way to being a top horse."

Baffert remembers Marlow contacting him shortly after Justify's arrival at Los Al and telling him they had a really nice-looking horse on their hands. "I asked him who he was by," Baffert said, "and Mike said, 'Scat Daddy.' And I thought, 'Scat Daddy? Why did they send me a Scat Daddy?' It sounded like he'd be a turf horse. Mike and I talk every week and I always ask him, 'Have you found me one yet?' Meaning a possible star. And he usually says, 'Not yet, but you've got a good group.'

"In December, I went down to Los Al to check out the horses. Mike and I will go down the line looking at them all, and suddenly when Mike came to Justify he said, 'You'll like this one.' And when I looked at him, I said, 'Damn, he's a Scat Daddy? Wow. He looks like a…man.' And Mike said, 'I'm telling you, he could be any kind. He's working really well.' And when Mike says something like that, he's usually right because he's been around good horses. He had Arrogate and American Pharoah, all of them."

Baffert was no stranger to Los Al. When he left Arizona as a young man, he came to the track to train Quarter Horses in California. That breed is built stockier and more powerfully than Thoroughbreds, which gives them the ability to push off with strength, key to success in sprint races. When Baffert eyeballed Justify for the first time, the colt gave him a flashback to the early days of his training career.

"My first impression was, 'Wow, he looks good,'" Baffert noted. "He was so beautiful, and his body looked like a Quarter Horse. What really impressed me was when you look at his hind end, he has the biggest hind end of any Thoroughbred I've ever seen. That body, it just rolls off his back. He was a little heavy, too, but muscle on muscle. He looked like a giant Quarter Horse, a really sturdy-looking one because he had the bone to go with it. And I remember saying, 'I wonder how far he's going to run built like that.'"

Throughout December, Marlow put Justify through a series of five-eighths works. Marlow sends Baffert a text at the end of each morning with a little comment alongside the time each horse worked in. "After the second five-eighths work, I wrote 'looked awesome' next to Justify," said Marlow. "Bob knows when I use the word 'awesome' that it's probably a runner. If I just say 'fair,' then it's probably not much, and 'good' is okay. Not too many get 'awesome.'"

Asked what sets one apart in his mind, Marlow stated, "Number one, they have to have good size and strong bone. They have to be a big, strong, durable-looking horse to dance the big dances. And he had all that. He had the look of a quality horse. I'm not bragging when I say we get a lot of good-looking horses, so when he first came in, it wasn't like, 'This has got to be a special horse,' because we get a lot of them that look good. And they're all supposed to be top horses. So you don't really know what you've got until you get to a certain point in their training."

The workouts put in by 2-year-olds at Los Al aren't official workouts in that they don't show up in official racing publications. And the news blackout was starting to get to Elliott Walden back in Kentucky, who was getting anxious about the progress of Justify.

"It seemed like he was at Los Al forever," Walden said. "I kept calling Bob to ask him if he's seen the horse yet, and he told me, 'Man, this horse is beautiful, and he can really run.' And I kept asking him when was he going to get him to Santa Anita.

And he said, 'Don't worry, he'll be getting over here.' And I told him if he had gotten him over there three weeks sooner, he could have started before the end of the year and we wouldn't have the 'Apollo Curse' to deal with.

"I would have really had anxiety had I known he was going to be a Triple Crown winner. But Bob has a certain way of doing things. I remember talking to Mr. Zayat [Ahmed Zayat, the owner of American Pharoah] and asking him about this Los Al thing, and he said not to worry about it; it's a good program. And I know Mike Marlow well from his days with Wayne Lukas, so I felt comfortable he was in good hands."

After Justify had worked three or four times going five-eighths of a mile, Baffert had the horse shipped to Santa Anita Park in January of 2018. It is not only a figurative transfer from the minor leagues to the major leagues to go from Los Al to Santa Anita, but it represents another hurdle that must be cleared as horses try to adjust to a very different racing surface.

Gary Young is a clocker who times horses as they go through their workouts in Southern California and is also a respected bloodstock advisor who has for decades bought horses for clients. "Los Al is a very good training facility because the track has a lot of bounce to it," noted Young. "Usually, when horses get over to Santa Anita, which is considerably slower than it used to be, they need a work to adjust to the track or they usually end up getting tired."

Baffert agreed. "They always get tired the first time here because the track is deep," he said. "They'll go a half-mile [four furlongs] and then sputter. So I finally got Justify over to Santa Anita and I started him off with an easy half, or maybe 4½ furlongs. [Jockey] Drayden Van Dyke was on him and he just kept going but doing it really easy; clicking off fractions easy. I have a walkie-talkie I speak on to the riders, and I said, 'Keep going,

Drayden.' He was still strong, and he went six furlongs in 1:13 and three-fifths just galloping."

Young, standing near Baffert halfway up the apron at Santa Anita, saw the massive chestnut blur go by, and asked the trainer, "Who the hell is that?" And Baffert said, "That's the Scat Daddy horse that Marlow's been telling me about for a while."

"The horse worked like a freak his first time out there," said Young.

Baffert made his way down to the track as he waited for Van Dyke to bring the horse back from the workout. "I was thinking to myself, 'Shit. Damn. This horse is serious,'" Baffert said. "I asked Drayden what he thought of him and he said, 'Wow, man, this horse is unbelievable. He's good. That was like nothing for him.'

"And that's when you know you have a really good horse," Baffert continued. "I knew right then he was a superstar."

Baffert being Baffert, he had to play a joke on his assistant trainer. After Justify had worked at Santa Anita, Baffert called Marlow. Said the assistant, "He said that he worked Justify that morning. 'I don't know, he's just okay,' Baffert told me. One does slip through sometimes who you think is going to be good and doesn't turn out. I was speechless for a minute about this one, though. I said, 'I can't believe I could be so wrong on that horse.' And Bob started laughing and said, 'That horse is just unbelievable.'"

Baffert played it straighter when Walden called later in the day, having seen on his computer that Justify had worked that morning. "I see you finally worked that horse over there. What do you think?" Walden asked. Baffert replied, "Man, he's a runner. This guy is serious." Said Walden, "I've been trying to tell you that."

Each major stable employs grooms who take care of three or four horses each and are responsible for every detail of their horses' day-to-day life. They bathe their charges, bandage them, brush them out, take care of their stalls. Baffert gave Justify to Eduardo Luna, who had taken care of Arrogate, and installed Justify in Arrogate's stall after Arrogate, who retired as the richest racehorse in U.S. history, went to stud. The night of Justify's first workout at Santa Anita, Baffert went home and looked up the horse's pedigree, trying to get a grip on the question that still hung in the back of his mind: how far was the horse going to want to run in his races? A look at the success of a horse's ancestors at various distances can often determine the limitations a trainer might be looking at with his current charge. Baffert wasn't sure, except for knowing that chestnut colt he had seen breeze that morning was something very special.

A week later, Young was standing on the Santa Anita apron overlooking the racetrack when Baffert approached him to let him know he was working the Scat Daddy horse from the gate that morning. Unlike a normal workout, where the horse is allowed to gather speed while galloping around the racetrack before accelerating into his work, a gate work commences from inside the starting gate, just like a race. A gate work serves to get the horse acclimated to the starting gate, and also gets him used to breaking from the gate in prompt fashion.

"To look at that horse," said Young, "he is so big that you assume he looks like a horse who would take an eighth of a mile to get into his stride. But he broke out of there very well."

Baffert was more concerned with slowing the horse down rather than asking him for speed, however. Thoroughbreds have to be taught not to get speed-crazy and spend too much energy too early in their races.

"I told Drayden just to sit on him and let him do it on his own," said Baffert. "He worked a little slow from the gate, going five-eighths and then galloping out another furlong. I think he went the six furlongs in 1:13 and change. Then I worked him again from the gate the following week and he worked much better, going six furlongs in 1:12 and change just galloping, and then going out seven-eighths ["going out" refers to galloping out an extra furlong after the official workout is over] in 1:24 or 1:25 just cruising. There was a race for maidens [horses who have not yet won] coming up at seven furlongs, so I wanted to let him go that far in his workout."

7

FINALLY, TO THE RACES

RICK HAMMERLE, FOR 15 YEARS SANTA ANITA PARK'S RACING secretary and vice president of racing, received a surprise visitor on February 15, 2018, when Bob Baffert walked into his office and shut the door behind him. It wasn't a belated Valentine's Day greeting Baffert was carrying with him.

Before leaving Santa Anita in late 2018, it was Hammerle's job to write races in two-week intervals that would be run at the racetrack, juggling races for different age groups and skill classifications so that the horses stabled in the barn area will have the opportunity to run at regular intervals. If a race draws enough entrants, it will "go." If not, it must be replaced with another race that attracts the requisite number of horses. There is a direct correlation between the number of horses in a race and the amount of money that is ultimately wagered on that race, and the more money wagered, the better for business.

Hammerle had written a seven-furlong race for maidens scheduled to be run on February 18, and that contest was very much on Baffert's mind when he walked into the racing office three days before it.

"Bob isn't one to come in always grinding away about, 'You have to make this race or that race go,'" said Hammerle. "He'll call once in a while to say an owner is going to be in town so try to make a certain race go, but he doesn't walk in here very often.

"I literally didn't know a thing about Justify until that morning when Bob walked in. There are always whispers about this or that horse, but I don't normally pay much attention to them. It was the strangest thing. He casually walked in and asked how the second race Sunday was going. I said I had three or four horses signed up and I wasn't worried about it. And then out of the blue he says, 'You know what, I have a horse in there that I think can win the Kentucky Derby. You have to kind of make it go.'

"I'd never heard anything like that before out of him. I haven't even heard him say that about a horse running in the Santa Anita Derby, let alone him saying it about an unraced maiden in mid-February. He said it very calmly, but with certainty. He got through to me in a few words and it struck home.

"So he gets up and leaves, and I walk across the hall in kind of a daze and repeat what he just said to a co-worker; then I called a buddy and said, 'You're not going to believe this,' and I told him, and he said, 'What are you talking about? It's a maiden race in February.'

"But Bob Baffert has the best eye for a horse around here, and to have the confidence to come out and say what he did—he wasn't shouting it from the rooftops, but he was saying it. And with that calm demeanor. He wasn't playing around. I've been around him for a long time and for a lot of big races, and I'd never heard him say anything close to this.

"So we ended up getting five horses. That time of year, our job is to make 3-year-old winners so that those horses can go into an allowance or stakes race, so I wasn't doing anything out of the ordinary. The race would have gone eventually, if not that day, then a few days or a week later. Looking back, I realize that

Bob knew the timing was such that it had to go that day to move things along for that horse."

On February 18, 2018, Justify was set to make his debut in that maiden special weight race at Santa Anita. A "special weight" maiden race means the race is run under allowance conditions, in which none of the starters are for sale.

Although Baffert claimed that "nobody knew about him" at that point, every other trainer and owner present at Santa Anita in the mornings throughout early 2018 would have seen Justify and noticed the striking horse, and word certainly would have spread, especially concerning a good one from the high-profile Baffert barn. And Justify wound up being bet down in his first race to 1-2, heavy favoritism in which a $2 win bet would yield exactly $1 in profit.

Before they go to the paddock to be saddled, horses enter a receiving barn, where they are checked over and the tattooed numbers on their lips read to make sure they're the horses scheduled to run in the upcoming race. Trainer Mark Glatt had a horse entered in the maiden race and was quite sure when he eyeballed Baffert in the receiving barn, a place he normally wouldn't accompany his horse to, that something was up.

"I looked up and saw him and said, 'Uh, oh. What's he doing over here checking his horse out for a maiden race?'" Glatt said. "I knew I was in trouble."

Baffert was still trying to work out a last-minute decision while walking with Justify to the saddling paddock that afternoon. Blinkers, which are attached to a hood that can be fitted around a horse's face, are cups designed to restrict a horse's peripheral vision. They are usually employed if a horse has shown a tendency to become distracted by other horses or the grandstand or infield, and they are thought to increase a horse's early speed by allowing him to focus on what is in front of him. On the minus side of using blinkers on Justify was Baffert's concern the horse not be too speed-crazy early in his races.

"I remember walking him up there carrying the blinkers with us and debating whether to run him with blinkers or not," said the trainer. "He walked into the paddock and was jumping around, feeling good; he's always a good-feeling horse. He was looking around at things. Drayden came into the paddock to ride him, and we talked about it. I wanted him to learn to break from the gate and sit back, and then come running. And if he was as good of a horse as we thought, he'd win. I wanted to do it the right way.

"Drayden said that based on his works, he wasn't breaking that sharply from the gate. So I decided to go ahead and put a little blinker on him."

The blinkers didn't do much to help Justify. When the gates opened, he broke last of the five runners from the number 2 post position. Show Time Rocket, Camby, and Paddock Pick contested the early lead, but Justify was having none of being left behind. He dragged his rider out four paths off the rail and blasted his way between Show Time Rocket (also trained by Baffert) and Paddock Pick 100 yards into the race. His trainer was none too pleased.

"He was laying perfect back there and then all of a sudden he got rank [a term for horses who get overly excited and rush themselves forward, fighting restraint] and just took off between horses," Baffert said. "I thought, 'Damn it, the blinkers were a mistake' as he was going up the backstretch. I had just run Axe Man [a well-thought-of 2-year-old] the week before and he set the same fractions and just stopped. And Justify is smoking along and I was so mad at myself. It was terrible. I thought, 'Why did I ask Drayden about the blinkers?' I knew better."

Justify ran head and head outside Show Time Rocket through swift fractions of :21.80 for the first quarter-mile and :44.37 for a half-mile, very fast splits for any horse, much less a first-time starter. At that point, Justify had established a clear lead over Show Time Rocket as Paddock Pick tried to close ground on him. With a quarter-mile to run, Justify had a three-length advantage around the turn and into the stretch.

"Turning for home, he's still in front but at that point I figured he was going to lay down," said Baffert. "But he re-broke and just took off again."

Justify wasn't laying down; he was putting more distance between himself and his pursuers without being asked by Van Dyke, who was doing a minimal amount of asking with his hands on top of Justify's neck. Justify came to the wire an effortless winner in a quick time of 1:21.86 for the seven furlongs. Track announcer Michael Wrona intoned, "He's a very promising type with the promise of bigger things to come. The gleaming chestnut wins by six lengths."

Wrona had everything right but the winning margin, which was 9½ easy lengths. Baffert rushed down to the racetrack, wanting to be there as soon as Van Dyke brought Justify back around just outside the winner's circle.

"I wanted to see how tired he was," said Baffert. "He was blowing [breathing hard], but he wasn't all corded up [tightened muscles]. Usually when you take the saddle off you can see they're all corded up. He was a little bit, but not that bad.

"Drayden was really quiet when he came back. He wasn't saying anything. He knew he was in trouble. And finally he goes, 'Uh, he doesn't need blinkers.' And I said, 'No shit.'"

THE COMPETITION AMONG OWNERS to acquire good horses has grown wildly intense over the past 15 years. The world has grown smaller, and everyone with the right equipment can watch any race live from around the world. As soon as a horse looks impressive in a maiden race, his trainer and owner can get inundated by a dozen calls from agents putting out feelers to see if the horse might be for sale. Promising young horses are said to have nothing but blue sky in front of them, and, like in the stock market, certain owners are more than happy to sell high.

With Justify's convincing win in the February 18 race, he created a frenzy that would make it difficult, going forward, to tell his ownership group without a scorecard.

Sol Kumin has made a huge splash in the Thoroughbred business in just five years. He got into the industry after hearing his friend and contractor, Jay Hanley, talking about horses while Hanley was building Kumin's home on Nantucket. The two of them hit a home run in their first at-bat when a filly they bought for $160,000 out of a 2-year-olds-in-training sale turned out to be Lady Eli, a superstar turf filly who won four grade 1 events and about $3 million. Since then, though, Kumin has specialized in buying various percentages of runners on the upswing, trying to get them after they've flashed talent but before they've won big graded stakes. Today Kumin, the chief strategic manager at Leucadia Asset Management, owns all or part of more than 100 horses. He regularly will own multiple horses in a single stakes race, and in fact owned parts of three horses who left the starting gate in the 2018 Kentucky Derby.

"By buying horses that are running, you know what you're getting, you can vet them, and you can do more work analyzing them," Kumin said. "We look at the speed figures and the ratings sheets and do our diligence—we'll talk to the jockeys, the trainers, and the farms where they were raised to find out about the horses and any past problems they may have had."

In 2017, Kumin bought into a package of horses owned by WinStar, China Horse Club, and SF Bloodstock. Of those five horses, three became graded stakes winners—Yoshida, Good Samaritan, and American Anthem, the last-named the one Baffert trained for the consortium. Although Kumin tends to concentrate on fillies, he has taken his shots on colts, and with good results. Exaggerator, in whom Kumin bought a piece, won the 2016 Preakness Stakes and that year's Haskell Invitational, both grade 1 races. He currently owns a slice of 2018 Travers Stakes winner Catholic Boy and the majority of 2018 champion 3-year-old filly Monomoy Girl.

"We're open to being creative because it's fun to have something on the Derby trail, and our program with fillies makes that difficult to do," Kumin noted. "We had done the previous deal with WinStar, China Horse Club, and SF, so we knew that kind of deal was on the table if we found the right horses."

Kumin said that Justify was on his radar before winning his maiden race because he had caught wind of Baffert's confidence in the colt. A few days after that race, Kumin was in serious negotiations to buy whatever percentage of Justify he could. He wasn't the only one seeking to get creative, however. WinStar had three colts who looked to be contenders for the upcoming Triple Crown season. Audible, owned by the same three entities in the same percentages as Justify, had just won the Holy Bull Stakes, an early Derby prep for 3-year-olds at Gulfstream Park in Florida. And WinStar also owned half of Noble Indy with a New Yorker named Mike Repole. Noble Indy, who was also bred by WinStar, would eventually win the Louisiana Derby. WinStar was looking to sell a package deal—15 percent of Justify along with 15 percent of Audible, to Kumin. In fact, WinStar insisted on making it a two-horse package. SF Bloodstock, which is more interested in breeding than it is racing, and with an eye on the bottom line, was willing to sell its 15 percent of Justify's and Audible's racing rights outright, while retaining its interest in their eventual breeding careers. Kumin decided to make the deal for 15 percent of both colts, but he wasn't alone.

It's not surprising that Jack Wolf also cut his teeth as a stock broker and hedge fund manager. Wolf got into owning horses around the turn of the century, founding a partnership group now known as Starlight Racing. At his first sale, Wolf wanted to buy a son of the stallion Harlan because he had made money on a son of Harlan named Menifee. So he purchased an Ohio-bred Harlan colt for $97,000 he named Harlan's Holiday, who went on to win three grade 1 races and was the favorite in the 2002 Kentucky Derby. Starlight has since campaigned standouts such as two-time champion filly Ashado, champion Shanghai Bobby, and grade 1 winners Octave, Monba, Purge, and Take the Points. But Wolf, a Louisville native, hadn't won the big enchilada, the Kentucky Derby, despite having started a half dozen runners in the race.

Wolf, unlike Kumin, specializes in buying yearlings at sale, although in 2014 Starlight bought into a colt named General a Rod the week before the Derby. General a Rod checked in 11th in the race and was injured shortly thereafter. In 2018, however, Starlight's crop of 3-year-olds came up short of qualifying for the Derby, and several of Wolf's partners in Starlight approached him asking him to find a horse they could buy whole or part of who might take them to the Triple Crown races.

"Around January I began searching," said Wolf. "We tried a number of horses owned by different people and just couldn't come together on terms."

Wolf had his eye on Audible, and in February he agreed to terms to buy 15 percent of him. When WinStar/China Horse Club/SF asked if he'd be interested in doing the same deal for Justify, Wolf called Baffert, whose excitement about the horse rubbed off on him. So Wolf ended up with 15 percent of the racing rights on both horses, the same deal Kumin had cut.

"It was funny," Kumin said, "we really wanted Justify and Jack really wanted Audible, and at that point it was easier for WinStar to do the same deal for both of us on both horses. So we each got one we really didn't want. But that turned out to be a win for everybody, since Audible went on and won the Florida Derby."

About buying Justify, Wolf noted, "When Bob Baffert gets excited about a horse, you can't help but get excited also."

For its part, SF Bloodstock was only too happy to take some money off the table by dealing away its 15 percent in Audible's and Justify's racing careers.

"SF is principally a commercial breeding operation," said its bloodstock head Tom Ryan. "We take great enjoyment in being able to share this experience with our friends, who showcase to a national audience the excitement that comes with being involved with horse racing."

So just to keep score, Justify, shortly after his maiden win, had four interests in his racing career: WinStar, China Horse Club, Starlight Racing, and Kumin's Head of Plains Partners. SF Bloodstock still owned a percentage of the colt's breeding rights but were no longer in on his racing career. While keeping the lawyers and accountants busy, all the action surrounding Justify's ownership had zero effect on how the colt progressed in his young racing career.

TWO-FOR-TWO

BOB BAFFERT AND ELLIOTT WALDEN WERE WALKING A HIGH- wire tightrope with Justify. Walden had sent the horse to Baffert because he believed Baffert, above any other trainer, had the ability to get Justify to the Triple Crown races on a schedule never before attempted. And Baffert was certainly thinking about the Kentucky Derby for Justify even before he ran him for the first time. The timeline for making the Derby, however, was unheard of, not even reaching the level of being iffy. It bears repeating that no horse had won the Derby without having started as a 2-year-old since Apollo—in 1882. Justify not only hadn't started at 2, he didn't get a particularly early start on his 3-year-old season either.

Because the Southern California circuit had for years suffered from a horse shortage, being isolated from most of the country's horsemen, Baffert needed to get creative to make sure Justify got another race under his belt at Santa Anita in the correct time frame, about a month after his maiden victory. While horsemen anywhere in the East could ship to a racetrack in Maryland or Pennsylvania or New York or New Jersey, for instance, to run, trainers in California who do not want to put their young charges on a jet have very few choices but to try and run where they are stabled.

Baffert didn't want an inexperienced horse like Justify to have to travel, and he also didn't want to step Justify up into stakes competition for his second race. The logical step would be an allowance race for 3-year-olds, in which the horses entered were not for sale as they would be in a claiming contest, and the competition isn't as tough as it theoretically would be in a stakes race. The problem with allowance races, however, particularly in Southern California, is that they are the hardest races to fill with a sufficient number of horses, and therefore subject to being replaced in the condition book if not enough horses are entered. And Baffert knew full well that if word got out that Justify was pointing toward a particular allowance race, no other trainers would want to run against him, and the race likely wouldn't go.

When Santa Anita's condition book came out for mid-March, Baffert noticed a one-mile allowance/optional claiming race on March 11. The optional claiming designation means that an owner could offer his horse for sale in the race but didn't have to do so. Neither Baffert nor Walden wanted to push Justify into the San Felipe Stakes, a grade 2 race for 3-year-olds to be run on March 10, and so they set their sights on the March 11 allowance event.

"I really needed for that allowance race to go," Baffert said. And so he entered a different horse from his barn in the race, trying his best to hide his real intentions and to not scare off the competition. In addition to that first horse, Baffert had another horse, owned by a client from the Midwest named Frank Fletcher, who he also entered for the race. Fletcher wants more than anything to win the grade 1 Arkansas Derby at his home track of Oaklawn Park, and each year he sends Baffert a horse with the hope of him being good enough to compete in that race. Baffert let Fletcher know about the one-mile allowance race at Santa Anita, and Fletcher agreed to run his horse there.

So Baffert knew that at least two horses would be signed up to help make the race go.

He told Walden to tell anyone who asked about Justify that the plan was to ship him to Sunland Park in New Mexico for his next race. He absolutely didn't want to go to that Plan B, but it was an option if the allowance race didn't fill. The assumption around Santa Anita was that Baffert would ship Justify to New Mexico for the Sunland Derby, a grade 3 race that awarded points toward entry in the Kentucky Derby. And that's what Baffert wanted the other trainers at Santa Anita to assume.

Just before the official draw for the allowance race, there were six horses signed up for it, enough to make it go. Jockey Mike Smith's agent, Brad Pegram, acting as a surrogate for Baffert, walked into the racing office at the last moment and told Hammerle, "I'm putting the horse in." When Hammerle asked which horse, Pegram said, "Justify."

"I played it cool," said Hammerle. "We drew that race first so that word didn't get around, and there were six horses in there. I remember thinking, 'Great move.'"

Back east, Frank Fletcher howled when he saw his horse entered against Justify, and he sent Baffert a text that read, "Thanks for all your help, but I don't think my horse needs to be running against the best 3-year-old in the country. Could you put him on the next flight to Oaklawn?" Baffert tried to persuade him that this would be a good test to find out how good Fletcher's horse actually was, but Fletcher told the trainer he didn't need to find that out in this particular fashion. With that defection, five horses would end up going to the post in Justify's second race.

Fletcher having called Justify "the best 3-year-old in the country" was a wild claim on its face, and just goes to show how word-of-mouth can spread not only across a racetrack, but across the country. Justify had done next to nothing in competition at this point, while other horses had accomplished far more. Bolt d'Oro, the best 2-year-old in California the previous year, was already a two-time grade 1 winner and was deprived of the championship for top 2-year-old in the country in 2017 only because he drew an impossibly wide post in the Breeders' Cup Juvenile, ran out in the middle of the track for most of that race, and checked in third behind Good Magic, who would be crowned the champion off that victory.

Other horses were winning graded stakes across the country, and Baffert himself had a horse named McKinzie who was far more seasoned than Justify. McKinzie was undefeated in three starts, including a victory at 2 in the grade 1 Los Alamitos Futurity and a win to start his 3-year-old season in the grade 3 Sham Stakes. In addition, he was a sentimental favorite of Baffert's because he was owned by Baffert's close friend Mike Pegram and Pegram's partners Paul Weitman and Karl Watson; and because Pegram named the horse after a close friend of his and Baffert's, Brad McKinzie, who had died the year before from cancer.

Still, Baffert was behaving behind the scenes like he truly believed he had a superstar hidden in his barn.

McKinzie was scheduled to run in the grade 2 San Felipe Stakes at Santa Anita on March 10, one day before Justify's allowance race. He was clearly a major prospect for the Triple Crown races, Baffert's most accomplished 3-year-old at the time. So when a reporter wrapped up an hour-long interview with Baffert for a magazine story and Baffert said nonchalantly, "You wanna come see the Derby winner?" the assumption would have been that he was talking about showing him McKinzie. There was something in Baffert's voice, though, that hinted at a twist in the conventional storyline. Baffert led the reporter out of his office to the barn next door and to a stall a couple in from the barn entrance. Before them stood the massive chestnut specimen of a Thoroughbred named Justify.

The two men admired the colt, playing around with his muzzle until Justify tried to get a little rough and assert his massive frame. Baffert struggled to push him back toward the middle of his stall. Justify was playful to a point, but he exerted his power and let you know he wasn't to be trifled with. His majesty, his imposing presence, made him fit to be cast in bronze. That moment in early March stuck with the reporter, who wrote of the incident, and especially the "You wanna see the Derby winner?" line, in a subsequent column, drawing initially the ire of the trainer, who must balance taking care of all his owners equally.

"You're gonna get me in trouble saying that," Baffert texted. "I was just kidding about the Derby thing."

After the reporter texted back his defense that he didn't think Baffert had been kidding, the trainer shot back a text moments later that read, "I wasn't. LOL."

Walden may have sent Justify to California in part because of the consistently nice weather, but he would have been disappointed with Mother Nature on this early March weekend. On Saturday, March 10, it began raining in Los Angeles in mid-morning and by afternoon it was coming down long and heavy. In the San Felipe Stakes, McKinzie and Bolt d'Oro, the two heavy favorites in the race, hooked up and engaged in a stretch-long duel with one another that included multiple times when the two came together and bumped heading for the wire. McKinzie finished a nose in front of Bolt d'Oro, but after a stewards' inquiry in which three judges examine replays of the race, it was ruled that McKinzie had interfered with Bolt d'Oro and McKinzie was disqualified to second place, ending his undefeated record.

The rains were such that the following day the Santa Anita racing surface was still officially listed as muddy when Justify walked onto the track for the fifth race. That the track condition would serve as a valuable piece of experience for what was to come later in the spring for Justify was on nobody's radar on this cloudy California afternoon. With an eye on the big races down the road, Baffert made the decision to replace the young jockey Drayden Van Dyke with the respected veteran rider and Hall of Famer Mike Smith, who had handled Arrogate flawlessly during his run of great races.

Baffert had taken the blinkers off Justify for this race, and although Justify was bet down to heavy favoritism—a $2 wager would return a profit of 10 cents on him—there were valuable lessons Baffert wanted Smith to try and teach the colt. Still concerned that Justify was too speedy for his own good, Baffert wanted Smith to try and park the colt behind another runner early ("rating" him, in racetrack parlance) so that he could learn to relax and conserve his energy before being asked to run later in the race. Also, this one-mile race would be contested around two turns, unlike the one-turn maiden race Justify had won. Having a horse negotiate the two turns of longer races is critical in their achieving success at the classic distances, and racetrack wisdom runs to "you never know until they actually do it."

Justify began from the outside post among the five runners, and when the gates sprung open in front of the Santa Anita grandstand, he started alertly. Smith expertly kept the colt relaxed and on the outside of his foes as they ran toward the first turn. Calexman, who had been entered in the San Felipe but scratched out of that race for the supposedly easier spot in this contest, made the early running and maintained a three-length lead into that turn, with Justify running outside of and alongside two other horses three-wide into the bend.

Down the backstretch Justify was running nice and relaxed and, without being asked, cut Calexman's lead to one length as they approached the second turn. With three-eighths of a mile left to run, Smith asked Justify for another gear, and the response was instantaneous. Justify shot past Calexman like he was sling-shot, and at the five-sixteenths pole he was already a length in front. As they passed the quarter pole, his advantage was three lengths. Hitting the top of the stretch, Justify switched his leads effortlessly (switching from leading with his left leg to leading with his right leg), and he was a picture of perfection through the lane as Smith sat dead still on him, no longer asking for anything.

Track announcer Wrona intoned, "He would have to race in outer space to feel less pressure...this colt of limitless potential wins by six lengths [officially 6½]." Then, with a nod toward the previous day's San Felipe, Wrona added, "Just who is the most talented 3-year-old to race here this weekend?"

Smith, interviewed in the winner's circle after the race, called Justify "Extremely impressive. He passed the two-turn test with flying colors. He has a great mind for a young horse and was able to settle and take a little dirt [being kicked back at him]. I was gearing him down at the end."

Without being asked, Justify covered the mile in a tidy 1:35.73. However, Justify still hadn't earned a single point toward qualifying for the Kentucky Derby. Those would have to come from finishing first or second in his next race, which would be a graded stakes contest somewhere. But with two dominating races in the bank, Baffert's early call of Justify as the Derby winner was looking less outrageous by the day.

9
THE WHITE-HAIRED WONDER

FOR THE 20 YEARS BEFORE JUSTIFY ARRIVED ON THE SCENE, from the late 1990s through the first two decades of the new century, Bob Baffert was, and remains, the face of Thoroughbred racing in North America. Other trainers have won more Eclipse Awards for being the outstanding trainer in a calendar year, others have won more races, and still others have tallied more purse earnings in a given season. But nobody has dominated like Baffert in the biggest events, as he racked up a dozen victories in Triple Crown races from 1997 to 2017, won three Dubai World Cups, and three consecutive runnings of the Breeders' Cup Classic from 2014 to 2016.

As important as his excellence in big races, however, is Baffert's presence, and his comfort in front of a camera or microphone. Horse racing for the lion's share of the 20th century was dominated by gruff, tight-lipped Midwesterners who didn't feel the need to share much of anything with the public or with beat writers from their local newspapers, reporters who were more interested in cashing a ticket than finding a scoop anyway. The sport lost further exposure when industry leaders in the years after the Baby Boom of the post–World War II era made the disastrous decision to keep horse racing off the new medium of television, because they thought giving the races away for free would hurt live attendance and betting handle.

While sports like professional football and basketball thrived by being broadcast into America's living rooms, racing went the other way, and in the years after the Golden Era of the 1970s when Secretariat, Seattle Slew, and Affirmed kept fans coming to tracks for the thrill of watching superstars, the sport largely disappeared from the public consciousness.

D. Wayne Lukas gave racing a recognizable face when he began dominating the training ranks in the late 1980s on through the mid-1990s. Lukas is well-spoken, well-dressed, and can sell typewriters in an Apple Store, but he was of, and firmly planted in, a generation that came of age before the 1960s and '70s changed the cultural landscape of America.

Baffert was raised by blue-collar parents who taught him the value of hard work, but he was also a child of the new culture that taught there was nothing wrong with having a big scoop of fun to go with that work. He was of the first generation that was as likely to enjoy hitting on a joint as much as drinking from a keg (he did both). As he came up the training ranks, the age of the stern, gaunt horse trainers squinting under Fedoras with a program sticking out from their side suit coat pocket was on the outs.

The line of demarcation for this new generation made his name in the steamy heat of Miami Beach in 1964. Brash, funny, quick-witted, and with punching speed not previously seen, Cassius Clay ushered in the beginning of the new breed when he made the hulking and seemingly unbeatable Sonny Liston quit in his corner after punishing the reigning champ for six rounds of their heavyweight championship fight. As Clay changed his name to Muhammad Ali, forced America to look deep into its racial divide, and refused to serve in the Vietnam War, two teams took sides. The older generation, for the most part, despised everything about Ali and the changing of the guard that he represented.

On many Saturday afternoons, however, their children, the generation of the '60s and '70s, crowded around televisions to watch Ali fight on *ABC's Wide World of Sports*. That he was a rare talent and to many of us the greatest athlete of the century was part of it. But we also reveled in his poetry and his predictions, a man so sure of himself that he bragged incessantly and then always backed up the bravado. The hard work was there too, although mostly done out of the public eye. The idea of having fun along the way, though, was readily apparent.

So it should come as no surprise that Baffert, who would hit the ground talking when he gained enough traction to have the cameras point his way, this wise-cracking, good-time Charlie with a mop of distinctive white hair and Arizona dust still clinging to his cowboy boots, was a huge fan of Ali's in his formative years.

In a recent interview in which he was thinking back to winning the Triple Crown with American Pharoah in 2015, Baffert said, out of nowhere, "I loved Muhammad Ali growing up and I wondered if he watched the Belmont Stakes when we won it. I loved everything about him, and when I got to meet him, that's the first time I'd ever met somebody and I was speechless. I couldn't believe it was him. I was shaking that big hand and he said, 'You ready to rumble?' That was amazing.

"And then I ran into him again. Jill [Baffert's wife] and I were flying to Louisville [Ali's hometown] and somebody was in my seat and he was leaning over getting something out of his briefcase, and I said, 'Excuse me, I think you're in my seat.' And he straightens up, and it's Muhammad Ali, and I said, 'I guess you're not in my seat.'"

It is a direct line that runs from Muhammad Ali in the '60s to Bob Baffert in the '90s, but also a long one that does plenty of curlycues through the Sonoran Desert of the American Southwest.

Nogales, Arizona, in the middle of the 20th century would have needed an alarm clock to reach the level of being sleepy. It is a border town just across from the Mexican village bearing the same name, and when Bob Baffert grew up there in the '50s and '60s, it was well before immigration became an issue on the Southern U.S. border. With just 6,000 residents at that time, Nogales was a place where everyone knew one another, and even through the '70s, the border was open, and kids from up in Tucson, an hour north, could cross into Mexico on a Saturday afternoon and drink inexpensive tequila in dive bars that showed *Hee Haw* on a TV above the door, and buy mass-produced "genuine" local crafts like blankets for $20.

One of seven children born to Ellie and Bill Baffert, Bob arrived in early 1953, and immediately thereafter his parents purchased a ranch a few miles outside town. Bill Baffert worked on the Southern Pacific Railroad as a cattle clerk before going into the Army, and indulged his love for animals when he re-entered civilian life, breeding and raising Aberdeen Angus show cattle for sale; and then Quarter Horses. Ellie was a teacher in town, and with the surrounding hills defeating any chance for television reception, the family relied on each other for entertainment.

There was verbal interaction and plenty of back-and-forth banter—which is evident in Baffert's wit throughout his career— and also physical dustups. Young Bob took to the ranch horses right off and had his own to saddle up and ride after school. He showed steers and lambs as part of the 4-H Club, and a few years later, after his father had built a chicken coop on the property, Bob started his own egg distribution operation, driving into town in the family pickup truck and selling eggs to the stores.

Baffert credits that impromptu dairy business with teaching him how to relate to people in a business setting. He was an able salesman and picked up on how to deal with others fluidly, all of which has come in handy in his current occupation, where clients have to be recruited, nurtured, and guided through the highs and lows of animal husbandry and the vagaries of racing horses.

Despite his success with chickens and eggs, it was the horses who grabbed young Bob's fancy. He'd begun riding at age five and loved the feeling of being atop them. A three-day cattle drive with Mexican cowboys over 100 miles when he was 11 cemented the romantic notion of being a cowboy in Bob's mind, and the men showed him how to groom his horse and how to ride after the cattle.

At about that time, Bill Baffert and his brother F.J. began buying some Quarter Horse mares together. Baffert's Heller was the first one they put in training, and she won a couple of local races before trying better competition up at Tucson's Rillito Downs. Young Bob began travelling to the races with his father, who started running his horses around the state as far away as Prescott up in northwest Arizona.

When Bill Baffert decided to train the horses himself, he cut out a strip on the family ranch and tabbed his son to become the exercise rider. Baffert's Gypsy (the elder Baffert put the family name on all his horses) was winning races on the Arizona fair circuit, and before leaving for junior high school each morning, Bob would exercise her, then serve as her groom when the mare would run on the weekends. Before dinner, Bob would spend hours rubbing horses' legs with homemade liniments concocted by his father.

In Baffert's 1999 autobiography *Dirt Road to the Derby*, co-written by Steve Haskin, Bill Baffert said, "When Bobby was 10 he was riding, and even then he could pick out a good horse.

At 12 or 13 he had the ability to tell me right away if a horse was good or not. He was just a skinny kid, but he could handle and break and gallop all kind of horses."

In the purest form of horse racing, and likely its origin, two people put forward a horse, each bragging theirs could run faster. More recently, in places like Louisiana and Arizona, these one-on-one challenges take the form of "match races," where a makeshift straightaway, often bathed at night by the beams from headlights of cars lining the way, serves as the racetrack. In high school, Bob Baffert began riding in these races, each owner putting up a hundred bucks, winner take all. He was light enough and skilled enough to suit the job perfectly.

Like so many others who eventually got involved in horse racing in some capacity, be it as a jockey, trainer, or gambler, Baffert had to hide his early participation in the sport from his mother, who considered race riding far too dangerous for her sons. That sort of early deception is nearly universal among participants in racing. Robert Masterson, who would own the champion filly Tepin, recounted his father rounding up him and his brother every weekend in New York and taking them to the races. Masterson overheard his mother talking to a friend: "They seem to have such a good time at the beach every Saturday, but I can't understand why they never take bathing suits."

Bill Baffert would bring a helmet, boots, and whip from the ranch, pick up his son at school, and drive straight to the match races. Bob began earning 50 or 100 bucks a pop when he won and having money in his pocket was feeling good to him. At 16, he decided he wanted to become a jockey, and at 17, he needed to ride in three races to get his license. When his name showed up in the entries at the track in Sonoita, a neighbor saw it, and Baffert was busted when the neighbor told his mother to wish Bob good luck riding that day.

Baffert continued riding after graduating high school, both in Arizona and out in California at Los Alamitos Race Course. At some of the bigger races around the Southwest, Baffert remembers first laying eyes on Wayne Lukas, the king of the Quarter Horse trainers. Lukas' trailer was bigger and shinier than anyone else's, and he had an aura of doing everything first-class.

Baffert returned home, attended the University of Arizona, and actually had a short substitute teaching career before going back to riding, and occasionally training, Quarter Horses. Behind his laid-back exterior, Baffert was a fierce competitor, and he took to heart a conversation he had with one of his heroes, the great Quarter Horse jockey Bobby Adair.

"I still really wanted to be a jockey," Baffert said recently. "But he told me that if you don't think you can be the best at what you're doing, then don't do it. I knew I wasn't the best jockey; I was average. And I quit being a jockey the next day. That was one of the best things anybody has ever told me."

When a trainer friend of his got suspended, Baffert agreed to take over his stable at Rillito Downs in Tucson. The first day he ran horses out of that stable, he won three races, including a stakes, and became the leading trainer at Rillito in his first year there.

By 1983 Baffert had moved his operation to Los Alamitos. Among his early clients were an Arizona car dealer named Hal Earnhardt and Hal's father, Tex; and Mike Pegram, who owned a bunch of McDonald's franchises around the West. After Pegram's father died in 1986 and left him with Thoroughbreds, the idea took hold to leave the Quarter Horses behind and get into the more lucrative world of Thoroughbreds. Baffert claimed his first Thoroughbred in 1988. Earnhardt sent him another from Arizona and that one won in California. Most of his stable was still Quarter Horses, but that would soon change.

After feeling his way around with Thoroughbreds, Baffert went to Kentucky in 1988 to the yearling sale and came home with a gray son of Slewpy for which he riskily paid $30,000 before he had found an owner for the horse. When someone asked how much he had in the horse, Baffert replied, "Thirty freakin' slews," which is how Thirty Slews got his name. Pegram ended up with Thirty Slews. Slow to come around because of various injuries, Thirty Slews had to be nurtured by Baffert and raced only sporadically. Meantime, Baffert gave up his Quarter Horses in 1991, switched completely to Thoroughbreds, and began winning stakes races with horses such as Ebonair, Letthebighossroll, and Charmonnier. In 1992, having finally gotten Thirty Slews right, Baffert sent him out to win the Breeders' Cup Sprint, a grade 1 race that was the trainer's first victory on a national stage.

Pegram and Baffert have made for a potent team on the Thoroughbred scene ever since, and their friendship is going on 30-years strong, fueled by laughter and plenty of good times since Pegram was there to bankroll his buddy in those crucial early years.

"You could see Bobby was a great horseman, that's the whole thing," said Pegram. "I could tell that because back in the day, at the Thoroughbred sales, if we got outbid, I'd see who bought the horse, and if we got the horse, I'd see who the under-bidder was, and in all those instances they were people who knew what they were doing.

"What I know about a horse, you can put in a thimble. I remember we were at Los Alamitos for the first time and we claimed this horse and Bobby said, 'Come here. You gotta feel this ankle.' And I said, 'The day I start feelin' ankles is the day I know I hired the wrong trainer.'

"Back then, we weren't thinking of this. You hear everyone say they want to win the Kentucky Derby. I just wanted to have a horse good enough to run in a race on Derby Day. I didn't see all this happening, but I think he saw it long before I did. At Hollywood Park in the early '90s, he looked around at the competition and said, 'These guys ain't got nothing on me.' And he was right. The first horse he buys at the sale at Keeneland won a Breeders' Cup race. And he had to work with him a couple of years to get him right. That tells you something."

Shortly before winning the Breeders' Cup Sprint, Baffert had met a Budweiser distributor whose rounds included Santa Anita Park. Bob Lewis had a daughter who was best friends with a cousin of Baffert's, and Lewis and Baffert struck a quick friendship, with Lewis opening the door to having Baffert buy a horse for him. Meantime, a Northern California owner named Bob Walter was sending Baffert good horses to train, including Cavonnier, who won the El Camino Real Derby at Bay Meadows in San Francisco in 1996. Sent to the Santa Anita Derby as a 10-1 longshot, Cavonnier burst ahead and won the race, sending Baffert off to Kentucky and the Run for the Roses for the first time.

Baffert was crushed when Cavonnier grabbed the lead down the stretch in the Kentucky Derby, only to be caught right on the wire by Grindstone, trained by his childhood hero Lukas, who won by a nose. Although Baffert didn't believe he'd ever get back to the Derby again, he had just agreed, days before Cavonnier's tough loss, to buy a gray colt out of a 2-year-old sale for $85,000. Named Silver Charm, the colt had little pedigree, but was a good mover. Baffert called Bob Lewis, who had entered into an alliance with Wayne Lukas, and asked if he was interested. Lewis agreed to buy the horse, and a year later, Baffert and Lewis walked into the Churchill Downs Kentucky Derby winner's circle with the son of Silver Buck.

That this young trainer from an obscure background could win the world's most famous race just a year after suffering the toughest of losses in it was a headline story. But as overwhelmed as Baffert was by that victory, he would take the ecstasy further still just one year later. At the 1996 Keeneland September yearling sale, Baffert saw a horse he liked and thought he could buy for $50,000. When the horse entered the sales ring, the bidding for him was less than spirited, and Baffert purchased him for $17,000 while wondering if he had missed something that was wrong with the horse.

When he called up his buddy Pegram to tell him he'd bought him a Quiet American colt, Pegram asked how much he cost, and hearing the answer, replied, "Does he have cancer?"

The colt, named Real Quiet, was too narrow to attract more money, but that didn't affect the way he ran, and for Pegram, Baffert trained Real Quiet to win the 1998 Kentucky Derby and Preakness Stakes, following in Silver Charm's hoofprints, although each failed to close the Triple Crown deal by narrow margins in the Belmont Stakes. But those victories for Pegram were deeply satisfying for both men, who had stayed best friends from the time they were driving pickups around the Southwest running horses at makeshift bush tracks.

Baffert's consecutive Derby victories brought him to the top of his profession, and the hits would keep coming. Point Given, whom Baffert trained for the Saudi Arabian prince Ahmed Salman, lost the 2001 Derby as the favorite but won the Preakness and Belmont. War Emblem, purchased for Salman's The Thoroughbred Corp. just weeks before the Derby, won the 2002 Kentucky Derby and Preakness. Baffert began dominating the California races for 2-year-olds and young 3-year-olds even when those horses didn't go on to excel in the Triple Crown series. He was attracting major clients and became a force to be reckoned with.

He also relished the attention and the spotlight. And reporters and cameramen loved him right back. Here was a star they could hitch their wagons to, one who was always good for colorful quotes and a laugh to boot. When the FOX network began televising horse racing in 1999, the Austin Powers films were at the height of their popularity, and Baffert agreed to do a bit on FOX's telecast of the Hollywood Gold Cup impersonating Dr. Evil and Austin Powers. After winning the Preakness he'd take the trophy cup given to the winning Preakness trainer, turn it upside down, and put it on his head in the winner's circle ceremony. Racing had never seen anything like it.

The fans loved Baffert's irreverence, particularly the ones who came out to have a good time at the important races. They treated Baffert's appearances with his horses on big days like he was a rock star taking the stage, which, in effect, he was.

All was not rosy as the new century dawned, however. Baffert's first wife, Sherry, the mother of his first four children, and he grew apart and their 15-year marriage ended. With success comes jealousy from peers and competitors, and Baffert's acerbic wit, burnished in those early days sitting around the ranch with his family, didn't always play well once he was beating others consistently. He began entering and then scratching headline horses in big races, earning the ire of racetrack officials. Baffert was a bit too adept at twisting the knife once he had opened someone with it and was resented for various comments.

At a post position draw for the 2000 Santa Anita Derby, he suggested to trainer Jenine Sahadi that her jockey, Chris McCarron, was actually the one training her horse. He compared trainer Sonny Hine to Elmer Fudd without knowing Hine had a disease that affected his speech. When asked how long he had known Lukas, whose perfect, pearly white teeth are not likely factory original, Baffert cracked, "I knew Wayne back when he had bad teeth."

The wisecracks weren't generally made maliciously, but one opens himself up to being taken the wrong way under these circumstances. Nearly everyone in very public professions has ups and downs to their career arcs, and any of dozens of actors a few miles down the road in Hollywood could have told Baffert that the same people who build someone up can, without warning, reverse course and try to break the same person down. Baffert understands that the negative feelings toward him at the time were partially self-inflicted.

"When you're winning, you're going to make enemies," he said. "And the bashing starts. Sometimes I'd talk too much and stupid things would come out. My whole life, my family has kidded around and made fun of each other. Most people realize it's a joke, but it's gotten me in trouble."

Added Pegram, who's had a front-row seat for the Baffert passion play, "Bobby went from being the darling of the media to having a target on his back, and he has to carry some of the responsibility for that. He's always been a competitive and serious person about his business, but people didn't see it because he was acting like a clown."

From 1998 to 2002, Baffert runners had annual purse earnings of between $12 and $17 million and won between 29 and 63 stakes per year. From 2003 to 2007, his horses earned between $5.9 and $9.4 million annually, and won between 16 and 31 stakes. It wasn't a crash, but there was definitely a downturn afoot, so much so that a jockey's agent, seeing Baffert at Del Mar in 2007, cracked, "Look, it's dead man walking."

In quick succession, major clients like Bob Lewis, Prince Salman, and Golden Eagle Farm's John Mabee died. California racetracks, beset by increasing equine fatalities, decided for safety reasons to shift to synthetic racing surfaces, which did not favor Baffert's speed-oriented program. Baffert dug in his boots, though, and the competitor in him fought back. And it should be noted, it was his oldest patrons who were rewarded. For Pegram, Baffert trained Midnight Lute to a pair of Breeders' Cup Sprint victories and championships. For Hal Earnhardt, Baffert won the Breeders' Cup Juvenile Fillies in 2007 with Indian Blessing, who earned championship honors that year as the best 2-year-old filly in the nation, and another the following year for best female sprinter. In 2010, Pegram's Lookin At Lucky won the Preakness Stakes under Baffert's tutelage. The horse was so named when Pegram, after listening to somebody describe some good fortune they'd had, pointed to himself and said, "Man, you're lookin' at lucky."

Baffert was voted into Thoroughbred racing's Hall of Fame in Saratoga Springs, New York, in 2009. Along with the honor, he was happiest that his parents, who both were fighting health issues at the time, were able to be at the induction ceremony. His mother died in 2011 and his father one year later. Baffert himself would have the health scare of his life while in Dubai in early 2012 training Game On Dude for the Dubai World Cup. Baffert suffered a heart attack in his hotel room and underwent surgery the following day in which two stents were inserted to open up blocked arteries. At 59 and raising a young son with Jill, something seemed to click in Baffert after his recovery. The heavy partying days had long since passed, and he developed a greater perspective following his illness. Tired of battling with critics over social media, he closed down his accounts. He grew less flippant and more considered in his comments. The combination of losing his parents and confronting his own mortality gave Baffert the impetus to make the most of his time.

Perhaps it is coincidence that the three best horses of his career, to date, came to him in the years following those tribulations. Perhaps not. But there is no doubt that Baffert did a masterful job in 2015 with American Pharoah, bringing the colt back from a leg injury that caused him to miss the last few months of his 2-year-old season in 2014. And, after four attempts at the Triple Crown in which he tantalizingly won two legs but never all three, Baffert ended a 37-year drought by training American Pharoah to sweep the series. In doing so, he set off a celebration at the Belmont Stakes that felt like Armistice Day at the end of World War II, with strangers hugging jubilantly. From the time at age five when he first got up on a horse, Baffert finally reached the pinnacle of North American racing.

"I don't think he would admit it, but there was a restlessness in Bob before he won the Triple Crown," said Jill. "That was a goal in his life and having been so close to it so many times, he felt it had slipped through his hands. Just being a part of that changed all of us; to be around something so great and so much bigger than we are.

"The biggest change with Bob is he's comfortable where he's at. He doesn't feel like he's constantly on the wheel spinning. Before, there was always a pressure to keep producing and performing, and while he still has that drive, I think he's able to be appreciative and grateful for his whole career."

Added Pegram, "Bobby has gotten more humble as he's gotten older, and after his mother and dad's passing. We're all getting a little older, but there's still that smile, and he still remembers where he came from."

Fourteen months after American Pharoah won the Triple Crown, Baffert unleashed Arrogate to shatter more than a century's worth of history in the Travers Stakes at Saratoga, which he won by a record 13½ lengths in record time of 1:59.36. Arrogate would then close from three lengths behind the far more seasoned and accomplished California Chrome to win the 2016 Breeders' Cup Classic at Santa Anita, dominate the 2017 Pegasus World Cup in Florida, and, after being left 20 lengths behind at race's beginning, somehow come back and defeat Gun Runner in the Dubai World Cup in one of the most amazing performances of the modern era.

"Of all my horses, these three are the best I've trained," said Baffert of American Pharoah, Arrogate, and Justify. "They're really out there, with Point Given in the mix too. These horses have extra gears they don't show you when they train in the morning. They do incredible things. To watch the way Arrogate ran down a great horse like California Chrome, and the way he walked out of the gate in Dubai and then runs past a horse like [eventual Horse of the Year] Gun Runner like he was tied up… And now this horse [Justify], the first couple of times I worked him, it was like, 'Don't tell me, I can't have another one like this.' And sure enough…"

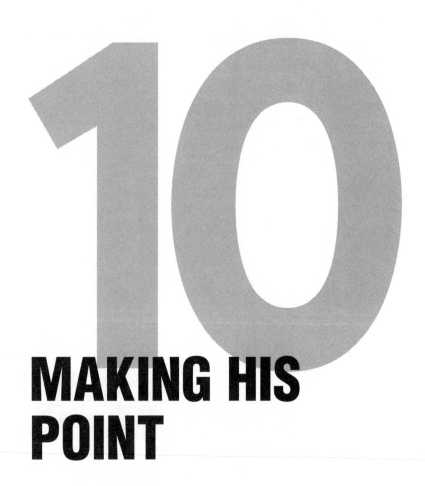

10
MAKING HIS POINT

THE GREAT TELEVISION WRITER DAVID MILCH, WHO FOR MANY years was also an owner of Thoroughbreds, includes some version of the line in almost all of his shows, and in many of his personal conversations: "If you want to hear God laugh, tell Him your plans."

In mid-March of 2018 Bob Baffert had three possible candidates for the Kentucky Derby. There was McKinzie, who had already earned enough points to make the 20-horse field; Solomini, owned by American Pharoah's owner Zayat Stables, who had some talent but raced erratically and seemed to lack the mental component to be a top racehorse; and the still-largely-inexperienced Justify.

Six years earlier, Churchill Downs had shifted to a system that awarded qualifying points for the Derby geared toward horses who won the important prep races that occurred closest to the first Saturday in May. This was a switch from the previous system, where horses who excelled at 2 the previous year and in earlier, shorter races could gain entry into the Derby. The new system seems to have eliminated horses who had peaked too early in their careers, and those who did well at shorter distances but would not handle the 1¼-mile Derby. Related or not, since the implementation of the new points system, the favorite had won the Kentucky Derby all five years, beginning with Orb in 2013.

Justify would have one crack at earning enough points to become eligible for the Derby, and Baffert was pointing him for the Arkansas Derby at Oaklawn Park in Hot Springs, a race in which the trainer had been most successful in the recent past, including with American Pharoah. McKinzie would stay home at Santa Anita and run in the Santa Anita Derby. At least, that was the plan.

Baffert remembers exactly where he was when the phone call came from his top assistant, Jimmy Barnes. Baffert had made the journey to Dubai to try and win the Dubai World Cup with West Coast, the champion 3-year-old of 2017, in late March of 2018. West Coast was training well up to the race and Baffert had his family with him, mixing work with a mini-vacation.

"I was in the hotel lobby getting ready to go to dinner when I got the call from Jimmy that McKinzie had injured his hock, and it made me sick to my stomach," said Baffert. "We were talking about if it wasn't too bad, maybe he could run in the Preakness. But he said our vet, Dr. Vince Baker, thought it was something with the hock, and I knew deep inside he wasn't making the Triple Crown races."

Just then Jill, a former TV newswoman in Louisville, got off the elevator, took one look at her husband, and asked him what was wrong. When he tried to play it off, she wasn't buying, and he told her about McKinzie.

"You have to call Mike [Pegram] and the car guys [co-owners Weitman and Watson both own car dealerships in Tucson] and let them know, because they're already psyched about the Derby," she said, telling her husband what he already knew all too well. "And you better hope that red horse is as good as you think he is."

Baffert called McKinzie's owners and told them the bad news ("I put them in the hospital," he said), then made a call to Elliott Walden, who had already booked trips for a large WinStar contingent to Hot Springs for the Arkansas Derby.

"I told him there's a change of plans, told him about McKinzie, and that I was keeping Justify home to run in the Santa Anita Derby instead of shipping him to Arkansas," said Baffert. "His stall is 100 yards away from the paddock; why would I put him on a plane and risk that when he's so good?"

Walden debated that decision with his trainer because he thought the Arkansas race might be easier for Justify, with less competition in it.

"He asked me if I was worried about running against Bolt d'Oro, and I told him I wasn't worried. McKinzie handled Bolt, and I thought this horse is better than McKinzie, and that we'll find out," Baffert said. "Worst-case scenario, if he can't beat Bolt, we could use the extra time and go to the Preakness with him."

Walden remembered being concerned about Justify going up against Bolt d'Oro. "Wearing a stallion manager's hat, I wanted him to win a grade 1 before the Kentucky Derby, because you can never count on the Derby being the time your horse is going to win one of those," said Walden. "There are too many factors in play, so the race before the Derby becomes a key race. I wanted to put him in the easiest possible race, but Magnum Moon [who would win the Arkansas Derby] wasn't anything to sneeze at either. Bob's confidence gave me confidence."

As much as his heart was hoping McKinzie would become a superstar, Baffert's head was telling him something different. When asked to compare Justify's way of traveling to his other top horses, he said, "Justify reminds me of Pharoah in that they both worked effortlessly, making a slow track look fast. Arrogate was that way, too. But the way Justify moves—Pharoah would throw his ears forward and reach out there with his front feet and a big, long stride—and this horse is the same way. And he carries 100 pounds more than Pharoah.

"McKinzie I thought was the same type. He works that way; he's that kind of horse. But this guy [Justify], I knew he was *the* guy. McKinzie is good, but this horse has that little extra that you're looking for. When you work him, he doesn't get tired. You can't wear him out. That's what it is. They just keep going without taking a deep breath. It's easy on them. It's something in their makeup—their heart, their lungs. He's a heavy horse that doesn't move like a heavy horse.

"He barely lifts his feet off the ground, like a daisy cutter barely touching the surface. He's light on his feet and has a lot of spring to his feet. Remember I was wondering how far he'd want to go? But he doesn't hit the ground hard and his motion, throwing those legs straight out, his feet don't come off the ground but a couple inches.

"He walks up there like he owns the place. He never frets. He's very imposing, an intimidating kind of horse. Even when he's just walking around, people go, 'Who is that?' Plus he's got that white blaze and that color."

Their travel plans altered, Justify's ownership groups made it out to Southern California April 7 for the grade 1, $1 million Santa Anita Derby, traditionally an important stepping-stone to the Kentucky Derby, and a race Baffert had won seven times previously. Despite his lack of experience, gamblers bet Justify down to 4/5 favoritism in the 1⅛-mile race, making him the narrow choice over Bolt d'Oro, who was held at 6/5.

Justify broke from the number 6 post in the field of seven and there would be no need to rate behind other horses on this day. Without being pushed by Mike Smith, Justify left the gate alertly and assumed the lead going into the first bend, with Bolt d'Oro running inside of him and two lengths behind going into that clubhouse turn. The first quarter-mile went in a pedestrian :23.96, with Justify doing it easily and not expending excess energy.

Up the backstretch Justify improved his lead to almost four lengths, doing it on his own and without encouragement from Smith. The half-mile split was a mild :47.85, as Justify wasn't being pushed by another horse to go any faster than necessary but was quickening on his own over a track that Baffert said was very slow. With a half-mile to run, Smith took a quick look behind him and saw Javier Castellano beginning to push hard on Bolt d'Oro, asking him for his best. Around the final turn Castellano was pumping his mount for all he was worth, and Bolt d'Oro got to within a length of the leader.

Justify came off the turn four-paths wide, while Bolt d'Oro cut the corner and began making an impression down near the rail, clawing his way to maintain his position within a length of Justify. Smith then began pushing on his colt, unleashing three left-handed strikes of his stick, and Justify quickly dispatched his competition, widening to a three-length victory in 1:49.72. Track announcer Wrona, sending the colt off to Kentucky, intoned as Justify hit the wire, "He is on a dizzying ascent to greatness."

Baffert, though, and Smith had seen a couple of areas of concern, as Justify showed his inexperience (called "greenness") at various times during the race.

"On the first turn he got out wide, then came back in; he was all over the place," said Baffert. "He was gawking around and wasn't going at full speed. Mike said he was having trouble guiding him, so we'll put a ring bit [various bits, placed in the horse's mouth, give the jockey different levels of steering control], which is stronger, on him."

Because the Santa Anita Derby draws a big crowd, the track opens its infield to patrons for the day, and up the backstretch Smith said he thought the horse reacted to something he saw from the infield, causing Justify to suddenly accelerate under him.

With a horse who possesses as much natural talent as Justify, sometimes it is easy to lose sight of the fact that he is not perfect, especially this early in his career. The problems described by Baffert and Smith could be deemed nitpicking considering that Justify had won the Santa Anita Derby by open lengths in only his third career start, a remarkable achievement. And in the process, he had defeated, relatively easily, the best and most seasoned 3-year-old (with McKinzie on the shelf) in training at that moment in Bolt d'Oro, running a solid time over a racetrack that was slow and not conducive to fast times.

Baffert was gracious in praising Justify and Bolt d'Oro for their efforts. All things considered, he was relieved that Justify had earned his way into the Kentucky Derby field, and also that he had done so with room for improvement.

Not everyone was sold on Justify in the moments after his first grade 1 victory, however. On the national telecast of the race on NBC Sports Network, analyst Jerry Bailey, a Hall of Fame jockey, acknowledged that Justify had been brilliant in his earlier races, but "This is his least impressive race of the three…You know what, it's hard not to go [to the Kentucky Derby], but I'm not sure Baffert's convinced he *should* go…I wouldn't make either one of these two [Justify or Bolt d'Oro] the prohibitive favorite for the Kentucky Derby off this race."

Analyst Randy Moss wholeheartedly agreed with Bailey that this was Justify's least impressive race, adding, "This does not in any way tell me that Justify will beat Bolt d'Oro in the Kentucky Derby. A half in :47 and 4; six furlongs in 1:12 and 3 at Santa Anita uncontested is a base on balls. Justify is *supposed* to win with a pace set up like that. In the Kentucky Derby, that's not gonna happen."

Baffert, interviewed moments later on the telecast by Ed Olczyk, presented a far less gloomy viewpoint than Bailey and Moss. "He punched his ticket to the front row of the Kentucky Derby," Baffert said, smiling. "We were hoping he'd run like that. He really showed his natural talent today, and this will really move him forward. He needed something like this race. This takes the sting out of poor McKinzie, who would have been tough in here."

Smith, also in a post-race interview, stressed that Justify was a work in progress who was still learning how to be a racehorse. Bailey and Moss, though, took their criticism a couple of octaves up from simply acknowledging Justify was still green.

"Maybe they were hoping he'd run like American Pharoah in the Arkansas Derby, just winning easy," Baffert said after he'd heard Bailey's comments a few days after the race. "People may have thought, 'He's a superstar, he better win like a superstar.' But he just beat the best active 3-year-old in the country, and I thought that was pretty good right there. Bolt was running, and the track was really deep."

Baffert sent Bailey a text that read, "Dude, what race were you watching? What else did you want him to do?" Baffert said Bailey texted back, "I was too hard on him."

In the space of 48 days, Justify had become a racehorse with his initial victory, stepped up to tougher company and won again, and conquered the grade 1 Santa Anita Derby, ensuring a trip to Kentucky and the chance to make history on the sport's biggest stage.

It may not have been the way Baffert planned it back at the beginning of the year, but he was heading to Churchill Downs with a legitimate Derby contender who had plenty of blue sky ahead of him. The trainer also knew the circus of expectations awaiting him in Louisville, and realized he had a tough job trying to manage them. But he took a measure of solace in the way the big red colt had gotten him there.

"He did it [winning the Santa Anita Derby] like a big old kid going around there," Baffert said. "I always told Mike [Smith] not to try and win by a lot. The less he wins by, the easier my job is."

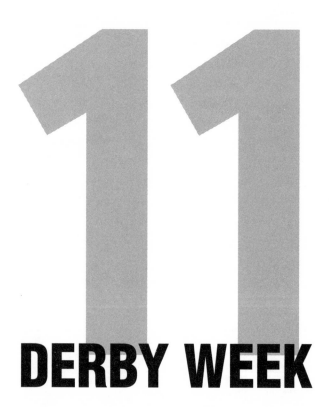

DERBY WEEK

THE DAYS LEADING UP TO THE KENTUCKY DERBY ARE A NERVOUS time. Trainers, most of whom ship themselves and their horses in from out of town, gingerly bring their stars to the racetrack at Churchill Downs, hoping they show an affinity for the racing surface, which can differ greatly from other tracks. They have guided their top 3-year-olds through a matrix of prep races, accumulating enough points to gain one of the 20 entry spots for this most important race of the year.

Now they must do their best to ensure their horses remain in top health, praying nothing goes amiss so close to their chance to have their names installed forever as a Kentucky Derby winner.

Racehorse owners, too, in the days leading up to the race, walk the paths between the barns and racetrack on eggshells, following behind as their horses stroll to and from their morning gallops. Many are first-timers at the Derby and are trying to convince themselves they and their horses truly belong here. Meantime, they are besieged by packs of reporters and inundated with dozens of details while trying to handle the travel, lodging, and ticket needs of family and friends. They worry about receiving a beneficial post position for their stars, and hope to hell their horses run well enough so as not to embarrass them in front of the world.

The fragility of Thoroughbreds has become a major issue in the past 30 years. Just as football players regularly leave the arena limping, or worse, so too can racehorses have one bad moment, take one bad step, and throw months of careful planning to the winds. There are no second chances with the Kentucky Derby. Horses are only eligible for it in their 3-year-old season, and if they are not in peak form on the first Saturday in May, the dream ends.

Pushing those nerves back below the surface, every connection of every horse may talk a good game. Everybody may convince themselves their horse is throwing off the correct signals that he's sitting on a big effort and won't be beaten. And every year 95 percent of them will be wrong.

Such whistling past the graveyard, though, would not explain what was going on in back of Barn 42 at Churchill Downs on the morning of April 30, five days before the 2018 Kentucky Derby. There, the imposing Good Magic, champion 2-year-old on the strength of his victory in the previous November's Breeders' Cup Juvenile, was busy tearing at a patch of lush grass alongside Longfield Avenue. His owners, trainer, and the bloodstock agent who had recommended he be retained rather than sold are most-interested observers. Good Magic had gone out an hour earlier for a powerful gallop under the historic Twin Spires that stand sentry over the racetrack at Churchill Downs. His gallop showed him to be enjoying himself, and he got over the Churchill Downs surface like he owned it.

Good Magic is indeed jolting his connections with confidence. Coming off a disappointing performance in his 3-year-old debut at Gulfstream Park in Florida in which he finished third in the Fountain of Youth Stakes, Good Magic was shipped to Kentucky. An hour east of Louisville at Keeneland Race Course in Lexington, he redeemed himself by firing a big race to win the

Blue Grass Stakes, historically a major prep race for Derby contenders. He looked to be thriving at exactly the right time.

Trainer Chad Brown normally doesn't do "giddy." He is an intense man in his mid-30s, round face set off by a crew cut that only emphasizes his serious demeanor. Younger than most of his peers, Brown cut his teeth assisting the great trainer Bobby Frankel, learning his craft from one of the masters. Ambitious and talented, he hung out his shingle in late 2007 and, after modest beginnings, started winning major races within two years. Brown has come to dominate grass racing in North America, so much so he had just four months earlier collected his second consecutive Eclipse Award signifying the continent's top trainer. He won his first Triple Crown race in 2017 with Cloud Computing in the Preakness, and he is clearly becoming a force to be reckoned with in dirt as well as turf racing.

Affable enough away from the racetrack, Brown is so focused while at work that he can walk past acquaintances without seeing or acknowledging them. He is aggressive and he is good, and his track record bears that out. His intensity can sometimes boil over after tough defeats. But watching Good Magic get his post-gallop bath and then overseeing his grazing session, Brown can't hide a broad smile, nor does he try. He joked about his newfound pull at Churchill, pointing to a brand-new sliding wooden bar that seals off the entryway at the corner of the barn. His gaze doesn't leave Good Magic, who is draped in a blanket post-bath, continuing to have at the lawn as he pulls large clumps of grass out of the ground with his choppers.

John Moynihan's countenance at that moment goes even more against type. A soft-spoken Kentucky native possessing a full dose of Southern civility, Moynihan is passionate about his work as a bloodstock agent, someone who recommends to clients which horses they would do best to buy, sell, or retain. He takes the responsibility most seriously, and rarely lets his emotions percolate over to the surface. But he floats around the grassy area this morning, bouncing from person to person like a guy with inside information waiting for the stock market to open.

Owners of Thoroughbreds are by necessity successful business people in their primary occupations—the economics of playing this game at a high level dictates participants have ample discretionary income. But succeeding in oil, automobiles, construction, or telecommunications has zero to do with knowing your way around a horse. Bloodstock agents are crucial to a successful entry into the sport, and a proficient and honest one is a necessary part of longevity in it. There are plenty who fall short of those bars.

But Moynihan's track record is sterling. As a young man he was fortunate enough to meet Bob Lewis, before Bob Baffert introduced himself to the California-based Budweiser distributor. Soon, Lewis was spending more and more time at the racetrack, and he entered the deep end of the pool as an owner just as Moynihan was starting his own agency. Seeing something he liked in the young agent, Lewis began doing business with him, and Moynihan and Lewis got lucky together. They bought a weanling for more than half a million dollars whom Lewis named Exploit, raced successfully, and sold as a stallion prospect for $12 million.

Everything Lewis touched turned to gold. He won the Kentucky Derby twice in three years, with Silver Charm in 1997 and Charismatic two years later, and also raced Serena's Song, one of the greatest race mares of all time and a Hall of Famer. Moynihan did the deals to sell those Derby winners to stallion farms, gaining respect and enhancing his credentials. Lewis eventually recommended Moynihan to Jess Jackson, who had made a fortune establishing the Kendall-Jackson winery in Northern California.

Jackson was having plenty of trouble finding a bloodstock agent he could trust. He had been fleeced and was in the process of suing—for millions of dollars—agents with whom he'd done business. Moynihan and Jackson couldn't have found each other at a better time. Jackson was building a showplace farm in Kentucky he named Stonestreet; following the practices that served him well in the wine business, he demanded everything be done in the best possible way.

Moynihan bought Jackson two racehorses who would become champions and Hall of Famers—Curlin and Rachel Alexandra—and bought mares to set up the Stonestreet breeding operation. After Jackson died in 2011, his widow, Barbara Banke, decided to continue building an elite Thoroughbred program. Having no interest in racing while her husband was establishing the stable, Banke fell in love with the sport through the exploits of Curlin. Banke today runs Stonestreet like a business, selling 75 well-bred yearlings each season. When Moynihan sees one he thinks is special, Stonestreet will go partners with a buyer and retain a percentage of the horse.

Banke, standing with a couple of friends from California outside Barn 42, was looking at one such special colt in Good Magic. Banke has continued to enjoy success at the highest level of horse racing, winning regularly prestigious grade 1 events at Saratoga and even at Royal Ascot in England. Although she still runs Kendall-Jackson, she also spends plenty of time at one of her two Kentucky farms, flying her Labradors with her when she comes to visit her horses.

Moynihan set up the deal in which Banke retained half of Good Magic after he sold as a yearling for $1 million to Bob Edwards. Edwards, a tall, easygoing guy with a recently shaved head, is also part of the giddy contingent watching Good Magic four days before the Derby. His stable is called e5 Racing, a play on his primary business, e5 Pharma, which develops drugs for both humans and animals. Edwards, based in Florida, had sold part of the business a few years before, allowing him to play in the sandbox of Thoroughbred ownership. And he has proven to be, like Bob Lewis, one of the truly lucky ones.

In his very first year owning horses, Edwards won the Breeders' Cup Juvenile Fillies race with a 2-year-old he named, tongue-in-cheek, New Money Honey. Edwards knows the odds against such instant success, but he hasn't yet awoken from the dream. Aided by another top agent, Mike Ryan, Edwards in his second year of ownership won two more Breeders' Cup races, one with Good Magic and the other with a filly named Rushing Fall. This is the kind of track record that has strangers coming up wanting to touch him so that some of his luck will rub off.

Edwards has an understanding wife and a daughter who is an equestrian, and so has made his dive into Thoroughbreds a family affair. His perpetual smile tells you this week in Louisville is going to be one long party, and why wouldn't it be?

Edwards makes small talk about Good Magic's season thus far. He works hard at the game, studying it to make up for lost time. Mostly, owners parrot the hype they get from their trainers when talking to friends and reporters, but Edwards has picked up a lot of knowledge in a short period of time. Moynihan came bounding over to the conversation, fairly gushing.

"It's so rare that you come into the Derby knowing your horse is as good as he can possible be," Moynihan said. "Chad has the horse peaking. We had Curlin in the same situation, but he got brutalized by traffic trouble in the Derby. But you know you're coming into the race with a horse that has a real legitimate chance to win."

"He looks great," said an observer.

"Have you seen a horse doing better than him?"

"Well, there's one over in Barn 33…"

The thought doesn't need to be completed before Moynihan's smile wavers, with vague signs of a grimace haunting his facial muscles just below the surface. He's been watching Justify all week, had also seen him out in California, and knows all too well what his horse is up against. But it's better to concentrate on your own riches and what you can control than to worry about what you can't. As well as Good Magic is doing, Moynihan knows deep down that he's likely going to need help in the form of Justify not bringing his "A" game to the Derby. And those things happen all the time…with most horses. The observer tries to ease the moment.

"It would be great, the two of them head-and-head coming down the stretch Saturday, wouldn't it?"

Moynihan and Edwards returned their gazes to Good Magic, trying to forget about the potential dream-breaker in Barn 33.

Not that he needs it, but Baffert at his barn at Churchill Downs rolls out the intimidation factor. It's subtle, but there on the wall of Barn 33 are the wooden plaques inscribed with the names of his four Kentucky Derby winners, three Kentucky Oaks (the fillies version of the Derby, run one day before) winners, plus the Triple Crown plaque for American Pharoah, who Baffert had here three years earlier. His barn sits 100 yards from one of the gaps on the backstretch of Churchill Downs where horses enter and leave the racetrack in the mornings. So there are plenty of passing eyeballs on those plaques, many from competing horse-men who will never know the secrets that are inside Baffert's head.

It's been 22 years since the trainer, who had bright-white hair even then in his early 40s, first came to Churchill Downs for the Kentucky Derby, enduring that devastating loss when Lukas' Grindstone nosed out Cavonnier. The lesson learned from that race is, while other trainers are happy to get *to* the Derby, Baffert is not happy unless he wins it. He has formulated what it takes to get a horse to the race in peak condition, while others fiddle about trying to figure it all out. Do you go easy with them in their training? Do you go hard on them? Jostled by nerves and their own second-guessing, missteps are common currency. It's almost not fair, someone having been there and done that enough times to know every pratfall. It's like a tourist to New York City who's been staring up at the tall buildings trying to outfox a wolf of Wall Street to hail a passing taxi.

What Baffert has learned, in his four successes and far more Derby failures, is there is no longer a thrill for him just getting to the Derby with a horse who is only going to get tired and dirty in the race. He would rather not bring that kind of horse here, not with him having to endure a week of answering questions and bravely pretending to have a shot when he knows in his heart he doesn't.

There isn't a better judge of horse talent—his own and others'—than Baffert, and he knows who fits in the race and who is here to massage an owner's ego. Sometimes it is unavoidable; if a client really wants to taste the Derby experience and has a horse who qualifies, Baffert, like any other trainer, must bring him. But he doesn't like it, and the experienced writers around him can read between the lines pretty quickly whether or not he thinks he has a legit chance.

Sometimes, you don't have to dig even that deeply. In 2010, Baffert brought the longshot Conveyance to the Derby. He was standing on the racetrack one morning when a horse got loose from its rider and broke away, running down the track at high speed. Every track has outriders—skilled horsemen on horseback stationed around the oval for such situations—and one set out riding hard to try and grab the loose horse, eventually collaring him not far from where Baffert stood.

"Good thing he wasn't riding Conveyance," cracked Baffert, "or he never would have caught him."

There is no ambivalence to Baffert this time around, however. Justify has handled his shipping from California to Kentucky like he has handled everything else in his young career—with aplomb. Nothing bothers him. After arriving in Louisville on the afternoon of April 30, Justify spends his May Day morning going to the track at 7:30, during a 15-minute span set aside exclusively for horses running in the Derby or Oaks. Reporters, fans, and visitors line the side of his path between the barn and the racetrack, incessantly pushing buttons on their phones and cameras to record the moment rather than experience it.

Justify walks past them like he's done it 100 times before. That he is this calm as a young 3-year-old, with just three races under his girth, delineates him as a remarkable animal in a sea of hot-blooded Thoroughbreds, many of whom can lose their minds over the smallest change to their normal routine. Baffert walks behind his charge to the track, his thoughts hidden behind ever-present sunglasses. Justify, under exercise rider Humberto Gomez and ponied by Baffert's assistant Jimmy Barnes, hits the dirt surface and trots off. Baffert and Jill stand at the gap, talking to friends. There's nothing to be done now. Baffert will not pay much attention until several minutes later, when Justify gallops around the clubhouse turn and past him up the backstretch. He is looking for stride and for energy.

Across the racetrack on the third floor of the grandstand, an army of 10 casually dressed guys armed with binoculars and stopwatches monitor the action occurring below them. These are clockers, mostly men, who watch and interpret morning workouts and gallops. Some work for racetracks, some work privately, selling their analysis to gamblers searching for an edge. Clockers not only time workouts, but rate them by seeing how the horse is moving and how effortlessly they are accomplishing their task.

Gary Young, who has followed Justify closely since seeing his earliest workouts at Santa Anita, travels to Louisville each year to watch the Derby participants prepare for the big race.

"Since Justify got to Churchill Downs, he's looked like Godzilla, like a beast galloping out there," Young said. "He is sound, he is strong, and he seemingly knows what he's here for.

"He handles everything so well mentally. Throngs of people are everywhere in the morning, and he walks on and off the race-track like he owns it. He never turns a hair, never sweats a drop. Between his gallops, his going over to the paddock to school [when a horse is brought to the saddling paddock days before a race to get accustomed to what he will experience on race day], there is nothing that makes me even vaguely waver in my confidence in him. I couldn't be surer of a horse going into the race."

As Justify comes off the track 15 minutes after he arrived on it, exercise rider Gomez gives Baffert a nod and a few affirmative words. The patron-lined walk is repeated in reverse back to the barn, where Justify is walked around the shedrow for 15 minutes to cool off from his gallop, stopping at several points to drink water from buckets placed around the barn. He is then brought out for his morning bath, attended to by two assistants who lather his 1,260-pound body up and then wash him down, employing a squeegee-like tool to get the moisture off him. Photographers incessantly snap away, trying to capture the water's steam as it comes off his chestnut body. When they have gone over every inch of Justify, the workers place a blanket on him. Justify walks around the barn a few more minutes before being returned to his stall. After checking everything out with his staff, Baffert makes his way out of the shade of the barn into the bright Louisville morning. He knows what is there to greet him: an army of media close in, digital recorders and microphones and cameras and note-books pointing directly at him.

"Let's get this over with," Baffert says, mostly good-naturedly. He will answer the same questions over and over again all week, but he knows the drill, and it's better than toiling away in obscurity.

"I think he looked great," the trainer says, answering the obvious question. "The track is real soft and he bounced around there pretty well; happy. It was a good first day, and that's what we're all looking for."

When a horse is doing well, his connections want to run the race right then and there. Three days seems like a lifetime to nav-igate, especially while holding your breath that none of 5,000 possible things go wrong with the star of the show. Baffert is dif-ferent today than he was 20 years ago when he continually played the jokester, but humor still breaks up the nervousness. When a reporter who had interviewed Baffert for a Chinese newspa-per (likely because of the China Horse Club's affiliation with the horse) comes forward to give him a copy of the paper, Baffert is delighted. He can't understand a word of it, of course, and the only reason he knows the article is about him and Justify is the photo that runs with it.

Baffert, holding the newspaper like it's an award he's just received, calls out to a reporter who has just written a long feature story on him in an English-language magazine.

"Hey, your article was good," Baffert said, "but it doesn't compare to this one."

The media scrum around him laughs along, and for precious moments Baffert has diffused any tension he's feeling and moved the process a couple minutes closer to game time.

Baffert has already done his serious work with Justify. Before leaving Santa Anita, he put him through a series of long workouts, of six and seven furlongs, like he's done with his previous Derby horses to give them a solid foundation.

Baffert's main task with Justify is guarding against overconfidence. He doesn't want to give off a hint that he absolutely believes he has the best horse in the race, even though he does. Horses make liars out of everybody, and you don't want to be getting cocky 80 hours before the Kentucky Derby. There are superstitions floating out there. Baffert in particular goes on the fritz if a black cat crosses his path. But he knows he's got the goods. This year, this horse has dragged him here. All things being equal, Justify should win the race. But racing rarely goes to plan.

"All the ingredients are there," is how Baffert puts it. "Now we just need some racing luck. We know we have a superior racehorse. He has a good mind and doesn't get too excited. He went out there today and acted like a pro."

That's as far as Baffert will go publicly in touting his horse. To the horse's owners, however, Baffert has thrown off nothing but unbridled confidence. Away from the media horde, Baffert said, "I'm not one to really tell the media I'm gonna do this or that. In my Quarter Horse days I did stuff like that. But here, I know I have the horse. When you have a really good one like this, I let the horse do the talking. I don't want to jinx myself. He's doing everything well. Still, you worry about them getting sick or something. There's no woofing until after you win. Those are the rules in my barn."

Besides, in the back of his mind, Baffert knows there's another hurdle coming up in a few hours: the dreaded post position draw.

Churchill Downs allows 20 horses to start in the Kentucky Derby, six more than race in most any other contest in North America. The racetrack receives a $50,000 entry fee from each owner, or a cool $2 million, which is exactly the total purse money it pays out for the race in 2018. So it encourages 20 owners to enter for the Derby. The problem is, 20 starters can't comfortably fit across the racetrack as they leave the starting gate, and the horse who draws the number 1 position, if he ran straight coming out of the gate, would run right into an inner rail about 100 yards down the track.

Hence, drawing that inside post position is a recurring nightmare for the owners, trainers, and jockeys who have worked to accomplish getting a horse to the Derby. Also, horses drawn far outside will be steered toward the inside so that they may save ground once the field hits the first turn. Thus, you have horses on the inside trying to squeeze to the middle, and horses on the outside doing the same. In a matter of physics, this causes bodies to bump up against one another—hard in many cases—and some horses get jostled about so severely that their chances to win the Derby are hopelessly compromised. Some get the air knocked out of them; some clip heels and lose their balance, or a shoe; others are shuffled back behind so many other horses that they lose significant ground they cannot overcome. Many horses don't like the kickback of dirt hitting them in the face and will balk instead of giving their all. And there are more horses kicking back dirt in the Derby than in any other U.S. race.

The post position draw is random. One official pulls a pill with a number out of a bottle, while another lifts a slip with the name of a horse from a file. That horse gets the post position inscribed on that pill. This year, the post position draw takes place in a large dining room on the second floor of Churchill Downs. Tables are reserved for the connections of each horse, with cameras and media ringing the back and sides of the room. Tension comes off the assembled horsemen like mist off a lake on a cool spring morning. Everything can go up in smoke right here, right now, three days before the horses even step onto the track for the race.

Chad Brown is holding court in the middle of the room, talking to the bloodstock agent Mike Ryan. Brown welcomes the distraction when a reporter joins them, recalling a conversation from two years earlier when Brown won his first Eclipse Award as the continent's top trainer, finally toppling Todd Pletcher, who has won the award seven times, including for 2014, when Brown thought he himself deserved it.

"He told me I couldn't win on points; I had to score a knock-out," Brown says to Ryan, nodding toward the reporter as the source of the statement. Brown is smiling, enjoying the boxing metaphor, but he has one eye peeled on the front of the room, anxious to hear, literally, the luck of the draw.

A scan of the crowd, and of the tables reserved for the connections of Justify and Baffert's longshot horse Solomini, indicates Baffert is nowhere to be found. Playing it cool is one thing, but skipping the draw takes that to a level of having liquid nitrogen in your veins. Yet the occasion is called to order with no sign of the trainer of the likely Derby favorite.

As the numbers and names begin to be matched up and post positions assigned, a racetrack employee takes a wooden plaque painted in the silks of each owner and with the horse's name on it and hangs the plaque on hooks on a giant board painted to look like the starting gate. Several of the desirable post positions are assigned early, and Justify's name has yet to be called. Brown is happy enough when Good Magic draws the number 6 position. Still, no Baffert.

WinStar Farm, the majority owner of Justify, co-owns two other horses in the race, Audible and Noble Indy, and so its silks, featuring a green, five-pointed star on a white background, grace three of the wooden plaques. With the dreaded inside posts still unclaimed, Justify's name is called with the number 7, and one of the WinStar plaques is hung on that hook on the big board.

Explaining to a reporter that they got stuck in traffic, Baffert and Jill saunter into the huge room just as the first half of the field has been assigned positions, and a five-minute break is called before the remainder of the posts will be drawn. Baffert, in his expensive cowboy boots and familiar, slightly pigeon-toed gait, meanders through and around a field of large round tables, looking at the board at the front of the room to see what he has missed. He sees the WinStar colors under the number 7 post position but has no idea which of the three WinStar horses has been assigned that slot until he can move closer. Finally, he gets in tight enough to see Justify's name on the plaque.

"We're fine with 7; that works," Baffert said, chuckling about getting to take in the big news all at once while his peers have been sitting and sweating it out for the past half hour. "I saw the WinStar logo there, but I didn't know which horse it was for. Yeah, seven's fine," he says, repeating the claim for a half dozen different reporters and cameras in the next five minutes. He's like a passenger on a plane who has slept through heavy turbulence, awakening only after the jet has made a perfect landing.

Baffert knows he's cleared the last big hurdle before the Derby. He just needs to keep his star happy and healthy from here on out.

One thing Baffert has learned in his annual treks to Churchill Downs is to release the pressure. The 24/7 grind of sweating out each detail before the Kentucky Derby takes its toll on many of the human participants, and it's possible the horses pick up on that anxiety. It makes sense that a nice, relaxed atmosphere around the barn can transfer to the horses and helps keep them calm. So Baffert takes a break. He is so proficient at his job that virtually every major stallion farm in Lexington, an hour east of Louisville on I-64, counts a graduate from Baffert's training program among its ranks. Two days before the Derby, Baffert;

Jill; their son, Bode; and Bob's brother Bill, make the drive to Lexington to visit some familiar alumni.

American Pharoah, the 2015 Triple Crown winner, has seamlessly adapted to his new lifestyle as a stallion at Ashford Stud near the small town of Versailles, just outside Lexington. He is bred to more than 200 mares each breeding season, which runs from February to June, and has helped foster a tourism industry in the Bluegrass Region that is modeled after the area's successful Bourbon Trail. Visitors sign up in advance to tour a series of distilleries on the Bourbon Trail, and it has become a huge tourist magnet for central Kentucky, spawning Horse Country Tours, an organization formed by many of the area's horse farms that has consolidated a number of small tour companies and put them under one umbrella.

American Pharoah is certainly one of the main attractions of such tours, along with the popular Derby and Preakness winner California Chrome. Besides his natural talent as a long-striding, fast racehorse, American Pharoah shares with Justify the attribute of having a great mind. Unlike Justify, Pharoah is almost human-like in his ability to embrace visitors and treat them with gentility and kindness, which is rare for a hot-blooded Thoroughbred. And even now as a stallion, when many horses get even more aggressive, American Pharoah is more like a puppy, letting people pose next to him for photos in between his breeding sessions. Baffert will always have a soft spot in his heart for his first Triple Crown winner. Before Pharoah, it was 37 years since Affirmed had last won the Triple Crown, and the achievement is a major notch in Baffert's bona fides.

The Baffert entourage next heads across Lexington to check in on Arrogate, who is completing his first year at stud at Juddmonte Farms. Arrogate had burst on the scene in 2016 after having missed the Triple Crown races. He made up for lost time

Elliott Walden (left), CEO of Justify majority owner WinStar Farm, made the decision to send Justify to Triple Crown–winning trainer Bob Baffert.

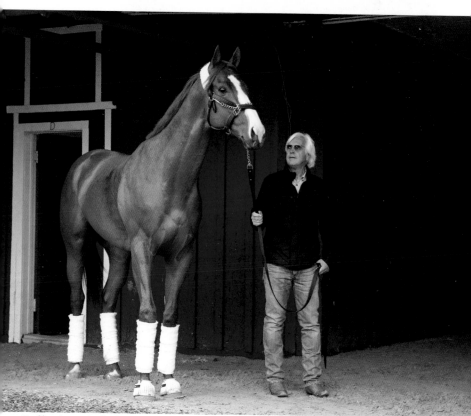

Baffert knew he had a special horse shortly after Justify arrived at the trainer's barn in California in November 2017.

"Big Money Mike" Smith, a favorite of Baffert's, was selected to be Justify's jockey following the horse's maiden race.

Baffert and his wife, Jill, have traveled down the Triple Crown trail numerous times, and they've accumulated the requisite number of superstitions to prove it.

In his third race, Justify held off Bolt d'Oro to win the Santa Anita Derby by three lengths. The performance made him the favorite for the Kentucky Derby.

On a sloppy track at Churchill Downs, Justify shines brightly to win the Kentucky Derby and claim the first leg of the Triple Crown.

Despite emerging relatively untouched by the Derby mud, Justify was favoring his right rear foot the following morning. The discomfort threatened to derail his Triple Crown bid.

After spending much of the Preakness Stakes pushed to the outside, Justify, down on the inside, has enough left to win by half a length.

Justify's victory over Bravazo would prove to be the closest race of his career.

Breaking from post position 1 in the Belmont Stakes, Smith took Justify to the front and never looked back. (Brad Penner - USA TODAY Sports)

The moment Justify wins the Belmont Stakes and joins the immortals as the 13th Triple Crown winner in history.

Smith celebrated aboard Justify after becoming the oldest jockey (52) ever to win the Triple Crown. (Dennis Schneidler - USA TODAY Sports)

China Horse Club CEO Teo Ah Khing (left), WinStar owner Kenny Trout, Baffert, and Smith pose with the Belmont Stakes trophy. The international component of Justify's ownership group makes him a horse for the modern era. (Getty Images)

After retiring with a perfect six-for-six record, Justify moved on to his next career as a stallion at Kentucky's Ashford Stud. His brilliant but brief career ensures that his place in Thoroughbred racing history will be debated for decades to come. (Getty Images)

and retired as the all-time leading money winner among North American racehorses. His gray coat is robust, and he is adjusting well to his new career, proving popular with the ladies.

Arrogate's exploits assured Baffert that there would be no letdown for the trainer, no slump following American Pharoah's accomplishments. Owners would still know that this Baffert fellow is the one to whom to give their best prospects. Arrogate thus was a significant horse for Baffert.

But likely the most emotional stop for Baffert is at the Old Friends retirement farm between Lexington and Georgetown. Founded by Michael and Diane Blowen, two reporters for the *Boston Globe* who decided to make a midlife detour into something they truly loved, Old Friends is a growing operation that takes in pensioned horses, famous or not, and provides them top-shelf care and paddocks. The facility has become one of the area's major tourist attractions for horse fans. Baffert and Jill have been major supporters of Old Friends, with Jill serving on its board. Three years earlier, the Bafferts had visited Old Friends on the Thursday before American Pharoah won the Kentucky Derby. Again, horsemen can be superstitious.

Among the farm's inhabitants is Game On Dude, who Baffert trained to an unprecedented three victories in the prestigious Santa Anita Handicap. He kept the horse in competition and cared for him until the ripe racing age of 8. A short distance away is the paddock of Silver Charm, Baffert's first Kentucky Derby winner.

Silver Charm, now 24, was a modestly bred horse purchased by Baffert for owner Bob Lewis for a bargain-basement price, at least for a Kentucky Derby winner. One year after the agony of losing that nose decision in the 1996 Derby, Baffert and Silver Charm prevailed, as the colt repelled late charges by Captain Bodgit and Free House to win by a head. It was the race that signaled Baffert's arrival as an ongoing force in the Thoroughbred world, and he hasn't forgotten it.

"First of all, and most importantly to us, Bob was very complimentary about how the horses looked and how they were being cared for," said Michael Blowen of Baffert's visit two days before Justify's Derby. "It was amazing. We had people out on tours here, and Bob spent two hours visiting the horses, signing autographs, and taking pictures with people.

"You can tell he's very emotional about this horse. He told [his son] Bode that if it wasn't for Silver Charm, 'I'd still be chasing horses around the desert in Arizona, and you wouldn't have nearly so much stuff in your room.'"

There is plenty going through Baffert's mind as he loves on Silver Charm, who was gray in his racing days and has turned pure white in the years since. Bob Lewis and his wife, Beverly, key supporters in Baffert's ascension, are gone now. Baffert thinks of them and his parents as he hangs out with Silver Charm. There is a good deal more perspective today, at age 65, to him than in his fun-loving, wise-cracking days of 20 years ago.

"I spend a lot of time with Silver Charm," allows Baffert. "He brings back great memories because I think of my parents and I think of the Lewises. I get emotional when I see him because here's a horse that didn't have the pedigree to win the Kentucky Derby. But he was a noble horse who fought hard. You knew when it came to a photo [finish], you could count on him. Whatever he didn't have in talent, he made up for in heart."

As he's walking back to his car, Baffert pulls Blowen aside. He normally sends an annual donation to Old Friends in June, after the Belmont Stakes, but now he peels 10 crisp $100 bills from his pocket and hands them to Blowen.

"You can only use this for beer and betting," Baffert says.

"Any horse in particular I should be betting on?" Blowen asks with a laugh.

"I can't tell you for sure Justify is going to win the Derby," Baffert says, "but I think he's better than American Pharoah."

12

HISTORY BATHED IN ROSES

OUTSIDE THE POPULATED CENTERS OF LOUISVILLE AND Lexington, Kentucky is a relatively poor state that doesn't grade out well in several key metrics. It ranks near the nation's bottom in money spent per child in education; and up near the top in obesity and opioid addiction. In the 20th century it hitched its wagon to coal mining and tobacco farming and has seen both go out of favor, becoming declining industries.

The Commonwealth has been more successful with bourbon, on which it holds a monopoly, as alcohol spirits have rebounded from a steep decline to where, today, especially with the rich, mellow taste of bourbon, business is booming. Purveyors can't expand production quickly enough and tourists are drawn to taking tours of numerous distilleries around the state that include a tasting of the wares.

Then there is Kentucky's love of sports, mainly college basketball and horse racing. The University of Kentucky under coach Adolph Rupp dominated college hoops before the integration of the sport in the 1960s, then famously fell behind the times, slow to shake the shackles of a backward-looking culture. The University of Louisville, quicker to adapt to the modern era, rose to prominence and today both schools are perpetual contenders for the NCAA championship in years that they manage to steer around rules violations. Passions run deep, and one man—coach Rick Pitino—has been at turns celebrated as a hero and vilified in each metropolitan center, having taken both universities to national championships.

Pitino has also, on a small scale for several decades, been an owner of racing Thoroughbreds. Kentucky, the birthplace of Abraham Lincoln, home to the largest underground cave system in the nation, and having produced Daniel Boone and Muhammad Ali, is tied closest to the horse. Because it is the country's capital of Thoroughbred breeding, thousands of acres of its rolling blue-grass hills are given over to horse farming, lending the state a unique beauty and creating yet another center of tourism that has vastly aided it and given it a positive identity. Developers, at least surrounding the Lexington area, have been somewhat slowed in paving over the region by protections for these acres on which new crops of Thoroughbreds are born and raised each year. The horse is still celebrated in the state in the manner it was throughout the country when horses were the preferred mode of transportation and a necessity in day-to-day life.

Kentucky Derby weekend is an unofficial holiday throughout the state. Run each year on the first Saturday in May, the Derby is preceded by one day by the Kentucky Oaks, the equivalent race for 3-year-old fillies. Oaks Friday is seen as the day when locals celebrate their horse heritage at Churchill Downs. Many in Louisville's workforce get the day off in order to attend the races, and some 100,000 turn out annually for the Oaks-day card, more than for any other day of racing in the United States outside the Derby. The fillies theme has been used in recent years to enhance awareness of women's issues and funds are raised to fight breast cancer.

Derby Day, though, carries with it a cache unlike any other. It is a seminal event on the nation's calendar of sports holidays, and with 144 runnings it is nearly three times older than the Super Bowl. While major team sports shift locales year to year for their championships, Churchill Downs, the home of the Derby, looms, along with the Indianapolis Motor Speedway (Indy 500); Augusta National Golf Club (the Masters); and the Rose Bowl in Pasadena, California, as the most iconic venues to host an annual sporting event.

Each year, more than 150,000 patrons stream through the Churchill Downs gates for the Derby, and millions more Kentuckians gather at parties throughout the state, at which barbecue and gambling are de rigueur, with attendees receiving a Derby horse to which their fortunes in a betting pool are tied. Such is the pull of attending the Derby live that half the fans who show up at Churchill Downs do not have clear visual contact with the race itself, not even counting those taken down by too many mint juleps across the length of the day.

General-admission tickets grant the bearer only the ability to inhabit common areas around the saddling paddock or under the grandstand in dank passageways that boast all the charm of a crowded subway station. Patrons can choose to spend the day in the infield, inside of the racetrack in a sprawling grassy area complete with facilities and betting windows. But from that vantage point, there is very little for the attendees to see of the actual running of the races aside from viewing the Jumbotron screen located high above the backstretch of the track.

None of that seems to dampen the spirits of the assembled, however. Fueled by distilled spirits and carried along by the promise of winning money each half hour as a long series of undercard races play out, patrons ignore the inherent shortcomings of their accommodations and revel in the Derby experience. Those populating the infield face the vast concrete grandstand renovated early this century to accommodate more well-heeled patrons in dozens of suites and hospitality areas. This massive grandstand now obscures, from most viewpoints, the iconic Twin Spires for which Churchill Downs is famous. The spires sit in the middle of the facility, dwarfed by the new construction as if they were the last holdout on a city street whose other owners all sold out to condominium developers.

Bob Baffert may have crossed all the T's and dotted all the I's getting Justify ready for the biggest race of his life, but some things remain out of his control, the most crucial of which is Mother Nature. For such a seemingly benign time of the year, when spring should be delivering moderate weather to the Ohio Valley, the Derby over the past 15 years has been run time and time again under adverse conditions. Some combination of extreme heat, raging thunderstorms, and prolific downpours has continually made its presence felt on Derby Day.

In 2004 a daylong thunderstorm of Biblical proportions put the running of the race in jeopardy before Smarty Jones splashed through the mud to win. Five years later Mine That Bird, a 50-1 longshot, navigated the slop to run up along the rail and shock the racing world. The very next year it was Super Saver, using the same tactics on the rail authored by the same jockey, Calvin Borel, to win over a sloppy racetrack. And making it three in a row, Animal Kingdom in 2011 won the Derby over a sloppy track. After a break of just one running, Orb in 2013 ran through the rain to score in the Derby.

Mine That Bird, Super Saver, Animal Kingdom, and Orb all won over what is described as a "sloppy sealed" racetrack, which will again be the track condition when Justify runs over it. When a prodigious amount of rain is expected to fall in a day, track superintendents will often "seal" the racetrack, whereby tractors pulling a heavy roller will run over the track, packing it down tightly so that rain will not penetrate the surface. This provides a more solid base for the horses. However, a sealed track represents one more unknown to the puzzle each horseman frets over. Will their horse take to the condition? The sealed track provides them one more excuse if their charge finishes up the track from the winner.

Although Nyquist in 2016 won the Derby over a track rated as "fast," it rained at Churchill Downs in the hours prior to the race. In 2017 Always Dreaming earned the roses over a "wet fast (sealed)" racetrack. Although Albert Hammond sang that it never rains in Southern California, lately it always rains on the Derby in Louisville.

So it was not much surprise that when Derby Day 2018 dawned on May 5, Mother Nature was once again crying on the city. The rain began at 6:58 AM and continued to pour down nonstop for the next 14 hours, setting a record for a Kentucky Derby Day and throwing one final wrench into the best-laid plans of worried horsemen.

"I couldn't believe the weather," Baffert would say later. "I was not feeling great about it. As a matter of fact I was leaking really bad; I wasn't liking it at all. I was preparing my wife, Jill, for a loss. We were ready to head out the gate as soon as they crossed the wire."

Jack Wolf became a local celebrity in the week leading up to the race merely by being a Louisville native. Churchill Downs' great director of publicity John Asher, whose death three months after this Derby would shock the industry, had dug up the fact that no Louisville native had owned a Kentucky Derby winner in more than 100 years, since H.C. Applegate's gelding Old Rosebud won by eight lengths as the odds-on favorite in 1914. The local Louisville media, which covers the Derby 24/7 for the week leading up to the race, descended on Wolf. His Starlight

Racing partnership that had bought a slice of Justify consisted of a dozen members, half of whom lived in Louisville.

Wolf's belief in Justify had wavered earlier in the week, until a rival trainer with another horse in the race sauntered up to him and said nobody was going to beat the colt.

"I changed my tune right then," Wolf noted. "And after talking to Baffert, his confidence spilled over to me. It's hard to believe, but I wasn't nervous on Derby Day. From doubting Justify a couple days before, now I didn't think there was any way we would lose if we got a good trip."

The Derby Day races begin in late morning, making it a long day for patrons and horses alike. Television networks have dictated that the Kentucky Derby, which used to be run in the 4:00 hour, now be contested shortly before 7:00 PM. Because of the first race being run at about 11:00 AM, there is little or no training of horses Derby morning, and nothing much left for trainers of Derby horses to do the day of the race. Horses slated to run on any given day generally aren't brought to the track anyway, nor are they fed the morning they are to race.

Baffert may have been confident, but he is also superstitious. Horse trainers know a thousand things can go wrong in the blink of an eye, and they prefer to keep on the good side of whatever spirits may be lurking. Bob, Jill, and their 13-year-old son, Bode, spent the rainy morning in their Louisville hotel.

"The nerves start flaring up Derby morning, and it was such a lousy day weather-wise, we just milled around the hotel," said Jill. "Both our families were in town so there was plenty of moving around from one room to another. There are some things we have to pay attention to. Bob is superstitious about having any kind of hat touching the bed. That gets his dander up. He doesn't like black cats crossing his path, and he doesn't like it when people come into the barn before a big race with the name of their horse on their hat. After winning a big race, it's okay, but not before.

"Bode has these socks from when he was younger that have shamrocks on them. He wore them for all of Pharoah's races, all of Arrogate's races, and all of Justify's races. They're so small on him now that the heels come to the middle of his feet, but we keep pulling on them like we need to get one more wearing out of them. It was like he was wearing anklets. I'm going to have to make a pocket square out of them or something."

Jill had no idea she was bucking superstition with the selection of her dress for Derby Day, however. Having two to choose from, she selected a green dress because the other one had intricate lace that she feared would be ruined by the rain.

"Bob could have told me not to wear that dress, but he didn't say a word," Jill remembered. "Then he tells the entire world at the post-race press conference that a green dress is a jinx and Justify had to be a great horse to outrun my green dress. My god. He was probably giving me the side eye all day."

Back in Lexington, Elliott Walden was making sure everything was running smoothly around WinStar Farm. It was a busy week for the farm, which not only had Justify, but also Audible and Noble Indy running in the Derby, and Yoshida running in the grade 1 Turf Classic (which he would win) immediately preceding the main event. Kenny Troutt, the owner of WinStar, was in town with a bevy of guests.

"There's a good deal of stress that week," allowed Walden. "But once you get to Derby Day, a lot of the details are behind you and you can enjoy it. We just try to keep things organized for everybody and moving in a good direction. It's great to be with family and with the Troutts."

A couple of times, the unrelenting rain slowed to a drizzle over Louisville, but not for long before the heavy stuff returned.

Walking from the grandstand around to the barn area 90 minutes before the Derby, the racetrack was a swamp of deep slop, the kind where you feared you'd be leaving your shoe in the ground when you picked up your foot for each step.

All was quiet around Baffert's Barn 33 an hour before the race. Over at Barn 42, however, a van was backed up near the entrance on the Longfield Road side of the barn, its back door open for easy access to supplies. A tequila-and-chips get-together was being enjoyed by staffers connected to the owners just under the barn eaves inside the rain, at the corner of the barn that housed Good Magic. There seemed no better way to beat the inclement weather and heightened nerves brought on by the upcoming Derby. Everyone was wearing Good Magic hats and spirits were as buoyant as they'd been all week.

Over the balky loudspeaker system came the call horsemen had been waiting for, in some cases all their lives: "Bring the horses for the Kentucky Derby to the racetrack."

The seasoned trainers do not immediately heed that call, knowing they have plenty of time. They do not want their horses to get overly worked up circling around with hundreds of people surrounding them for any longer than they need to. There will be enough opportunity for the horses to get excited on the walkover and then in the close quarters of the saddling paddock, with hundreds more people milling around a very small area. There is also the grandstand and infield with 150,000 excited fans who will further test the mental capacity of the Derby horses and the hot-blooded nature of the Thoroughbred. Many horses lose the Derby well before the gates open for the start. You can see lathery sweat gather along their necks and front quarters as they begin to overheat from all these stimuli, and they expend far too much energy before the race begins.

About 45 minutes before the Derby, the 20 equine participants are walked from their barns to a strip of the racetrack just off
the main oval called the chute. Most of their owners mill around,
ready for the walkover, which has become part of the Derby experience. Soon the parade will begin, and each horse surrounded
by his trainer, staff, owners, and entourage starts to walk around
the clubhouse turn of Churchill Downs. To their left are fans
behind a cyclone fence who have been sitting in lawn chairs and
at picnic tables all day. They scream at both their favorites and at
their favorite targets, horses and humans alike. Farther into the
bend the parade passes tents set up for corporate clients, and then
numerous elevated platforms for local and national TV reporters,
with bright lights shining upon freshly made-up talent.

And then, as the turn keeps bending toward the right, the
giant Churchill Downs grandstand fills the line of sight, jam-
packed with patrons. The cascade of sound pounds down from
the multiple levels to the racetrack, and now chills run down the
spine of the connections of these horses. Now it hits them that
this is the Kentucky Derby and there is no other setting like it,
and they are fortunate enough to have one of the 20 horses—out
of a foal crop of more than 22,000—to make it to the starting
gate. Ninety-five percent of them will go home that night disappointed at having lost the race. None, however, will forget the
feeling of walking around the Churchill Downs track in front of
that grandstand with waves of pure energy crashing down upon
them.

Baffert has done this walk enough times that he doesn't need
to ruin his shoes and clothes by splashing through the slop again.
His staff is top-notch, headed by Barnes, and Baffert will greet his
horse in the saddling paddock after the horses reach the grandstand and walk through a short tunnel. Once in the paddock,

they will be walked some more and eventually have their saddles applied.

In addition to Justify, Baffert has Solomini in the race. Solomini is owned by Ahmed Zayat and his family, who three years earlier had enjoyed the thrill of watching their American Pharoah win the Kentucky Derby en route to sweeping the Triple Crown. This time, however, their colt is being held at odds of nearly 63-1, and not many are signing up to try and cash in on that bargain.

Justify was receiving most of the bettors' love at the windows, but there were plenty of gamblers lining up to bet against him, hoping that the hype surrounding him was just that. His odds would settle at just under 3-1, the exact same odds at which American Pharoah had been held three years earlier. Surprisingly, My Boy Jack, who had run almost exclusively on grass as a 2-year-old but had won the Southwest Stakes and Lexington Stakes, both grade 3 races on dirt, wound up the second-choice at 6-1. Another versatile horse, Mendelssohn, a U.S.-bred who had also raced in Dubai and Europe, was also 6-1. Mendelssohn had journeyed to America and won the Breeders' Cup Juvenile Turf, a grade 1 race, to cap his 2-year-old season, and had also won on the dirt in Dubai in graded company.

The Florida Derby has been successfully graduating its winners to springboard to success in the Derby in recent years. Always Dreaming, Nyquist, Orb, and Big Brown had all pulled off the Florida Derby/Kentucky Derby double in the past 10 years, and Audible, the 2018 Florida Derby victor in whom Jack Wolf and Sol Kumin had each bought 15 percent, was given a big chance at Churchill, sent off at 7-1. Bolt d'Oro still had his believers. Brilliant as a 2-year-old, he was a grade 2 winner at 3, and his backers were still willing to think that he could somehow make up those three lengths by which he had lost the Santa Anita

Derby to Justify. He was 8-1 in the Derby. Good Magic was bet to the tune of 9-1. The impressive winner of the Blue Grass Stakes at Keeneland deserved heavier backing, but certain players realized that the Blue Grass winner had not come back to win the Derby in 27 years, since Strike the Gold pulled off the double in 1991.

Other recent stakes winners being saddled for the Derby included the Lukas-trained Bravazo, who had taken the grade 2 Risen Star Stakes in February; Enticed, winner of the Gotham Stakes, a grade 3 event in New York; Firenze Fire, who had been outstanding at 2 in winning the grade 1 Champagne Stakes and grade 3 Sanford Stakes in New York; Flameaway, a grade 3 winner in Florida; Free Drop Billy, looking to regain the form he'd flashed in taking the grade 1 Breeders' Futurity at Keeneland the previous autumn; the undefeated Magnum Moon, perfect in four starts including a four-length victory in the grade 1 Arkansas Derby; Noble Indy, co-owned by WinStar Farm and the winner of the grade 2 Louisiana Derby; grade 2 Fountain of Youth Stakes winner Promises Fulfilled; and the Gunther-bred Vino Rosso, who had been raised in the same field as Justify at Glennwood Farm and had won the prestigious Wood Memorial in New York.

The weather wasn't the only thing giving Baffert doubts as the Derby approached. During the week at Churchill, Baffert's horses hadn't been running very well. Abel Tasman, who had won the Kentucky Oaks a year earlier, had lost the day before Justify's Derby, finishing fourth in the La Troienne Stakes.

"I was having a tough week," Baffert allowed. "My father-in-law asked if we had forgotten to put deodorant on because we were stinking up the place. It was torture watching Abel Tasman get beat. And then early on Derby Day, we had a couple of chances and did nothing. Hoppertunity ran fourth in the Alysheba Stakes and Restoring Hope 12th in the Pat Day Mile. But then back at

Santa Anita we unleashed a filly for the first time and she won by 10 lengths. So I was starting to think maybe we were turning it around."

While his other horses weren't performing up to standards, Baffert could take solace in the behavior of his big chestnut colt, who was cool despite all the heightened activity going on around him in the Derby paddock. And then jockey Mike Smith, wearing the white and green WinStar Farm silks, strode up to stall number 7.

Smith is no stranger to the pressure of riding in the Kentucky Derby. He's had 20 mounts in the race, winning it in 2005 with a brilliant ride weaving his way through traffic from 18th place aboard 50-1 longshot Giacomo. His veteran presence and vast experience are why Baffert has tabbed him to ride many of his top horses in recent years. But being a veteran doesn't mean you don't feel nerves on Derby Day. Riders have for many decades gotten emotional when riding their mounts out onto the racetrack for the Derby and hearing 150,000 fans singing "My Old Kentucky Home," a Stephen Foster–penned ode to 19th century Kentucky life and being displaced from one's homeland. Like their horses reacting to the hubbub surrounding them, jockeys, too, can lose their composure in all the emotion, plus what is potentially at stake for them career-wise if they can win the race.

In 2012, owner Paul Reddam made the controversial decision to keep a young jockey named Mario Gutierrez aboard his Derby contender I'll Have Another. Gutierrez had never so much as seen Churchill Downs before that week, much less ridden in the Kentucky Derby. When asked about his choice of riders, Reddam explained why he had remained loyal to Gutierrez, who had won the Santa Anita Derby with the horse.

"When they begin playing 'My Old Kentucky Home,'" said Reddam, "Mario isn't going to know enough to get nervous."

From the tough number 19 post position, Gutierrez masterfully placed I'll Have Another mid-pack in the clear on the outside and rode a perfect race, taking the Derby by 1½ lengths at odds of 15-1.

Said Smith, "You can't treat the Derby like it's just any other day. If you think it's just another race, there's something wrong with you. Certainly, there are butterflies. Riding in the Derby is why we all do this. If you don't feel that way, what the hell are you doing this for? But having been around for a while, you try to harness your feelings and use that energy to your advantage instead of having it become destructive to what you're trying to do."

However Smith was able to wrestle his emotions, it worked when he walked into the paddock and approached Baffert.

"Mike was really cool," said Baffert. "You can tell when your jockey is a little bit nervous, and that's not good. So Mike walked in there, and we had a little game plan worked out. But it was all based on getting out of the gate well. If we didn't get out of the gate well, we might as well start heading home."

Trainer Chad Brown stood ramrod straight in the saddling stall reserved for the number 6 horse in the Derby, Good Magic. The gleaming colt was still throwing off all the right signals, and Brown's assistants led the colt into the stall, awaiting the valet who would shortly arrive with the saddlecloth and jockey Jose Ortiz's saddle, which would be set on Good Magic's broad back and cinched under his stomach.

Right next door Baffert accepted the arrival of Justify to stall 7. Brown stole a quick glance over the wood wall that separated the two camps.

"Everyone knew Justify was the favorite, that he came into the Derby highly regarded and with a flawless record, and that he was the horse to beat," said Brown months later. "But even after watching him train all week leading up to the race, my first moment of, 'Wow, this is a tall order,' came right before I put the saddle on Good Magic. They brought Justify into the next stall and he stood there like a statue. And I remember looking over at him and thinking, 'Oh, shit, this horse is the real deal. This is a magnificent specimen.'

"He looked like a chiseled sculpture of a horse. He actually seemed like a boxer with a chiseled body that just took his robe off in the ring and was dancing in his corner, ready to fight you. At that point, I was concerned about the task at hand, I'll tell you that. I think I know horses well, and I have respect and admiration for special horses. And his focus, his physical appearance; the horse couldn't have possibly looked better or more ready. I just put the saddle on Good Magic and said my prayers."

Dale Romans, a second-generation trainer based at Churchill Downs, announced to everyone Derby week that his horse Promises Fulfilled would be going to the lead in the Derby. Promises Fulfilled is the poster child for a talented horse who nevertheless is far better at shorter distances than he is at the Derby distance of 1¼ miles. Many such fast horses try the Derby because they've earned a spot in the starting gate, and you do have to be in it to win it. But the deck is stacked against them. Promises Fulfilled, since running in the Derby, has fulfilled his promise at shorter distances, winning the grade 1 H. Allen Jerkens Stakes at Saratoga at seven furlongs, the grade 2 Phoenix Stakes at Keeneland at six furlongs, and the grade 3 Amsterdam Stakes at 6½ furlongs at Saratoga, earning $535,000 in those three races alone.

Romans wasn't bluffing about his horse flying from the start in the Derby. Jockey Corey Lanerie sent Promises Fulfilled straight to the lead from his number 3 post position when the Kentucky Derby gates opened at 6:52 PM. Four gates farther out,

Smith got Justify away in good order. Justify raced to the outside of Promises Fulfilled, half a length behind him. Horses don't enjoy having mud kicked back into their face any more than do humans, and in the 20-horse stampede that is the Derby, any horse behind the frontrunners on this sloppy racetrack was going to eat plenty of it and have their chances compromised.

On the other hand, pace makes the race. A mile and a quarter was longer than any of these horses had been asked to run before, and going too fast too early is a recipe for disaster when the last quarter-mile rolls around and the gas tank hits empty.

Perhaps spurred on by the roar of the crowd, Promises Fulfilled wasn't much concerned with what was coming farther down the road. He lit out down the straightaway past the grandstand and under the finish line for the first time, racing toward the clubhouse turn in a very rapid :22.24 for the first quarter-mile. He then clicked off the first half-mile in an equally ambitious :45.77. In fact, he ran the fastest first half-mile in Derby history. Justify, glued to the leader's outside, was keeping virtually the same quick pace. In this, he was also being prompted by Victor Espinoza, the rider who had guided American Pharoah through the Triple Crown. Espinoza, here aboard Bolt d'Oro, positioned his horse just to the outside of Justify, which would have encouraged Justify to keep motoring instead of being able to relax a bit. Good Magic was drafting in behind Justify and to his inside.

Baffert usually likes to watch the Churchill Downs races while standing in the empty saddling paddock after all the horses and people have cleared out and headed for their seats. But today, the large monitor mounted high above the saddling stalls goes unwatched. Because of the rain, Baffert and his family are watching from a horseman's lounge just off the paddock as the Derby unfolds.

"There were two things I was worried about. The first was if the track had started to dry out, because it gets like peanut butter, really sticky. That's when it's the worst," Baffert said. "But the rain kept coming down, so it likely wasn't drying much. The other thing was the break. The break is so important. And he broke well, and then Good Magic came to him and tried to push on him a little bit leaving there. But Mike got him away from there really quick."

Maybe too quick.

"When I saw the :22 and change, I thought, 'Oh, boy. No good. They're smoking,'" Baffert said. "And then I said to Jill, 'Well, the second quarter they at least slowed it down to :46 and change,' and she said, 'No, that's :45 and change.' That's not good. I was like, 'This poor horse. He's going to lay down. There's no way.' You fret all week trying to get this big horse to the race. It's like having LeBron James on your team. You better win a championship with him. That's the way we feel."

Walden, a retired trainer, reacted similarly watching the early fractions flash up on the infield toteboard.

"After I saw :22 and :45, I gave up on him," Walden admitted. "When they hit the half-mile pole, I started watching Audible. I thought back to [WinStar-owned] Bodemeister and all the other Derby horses that had gone that fast and weren't able to hold it together. So I looked for Audible, because I thought he had a really big chance, too."

"He [Justify] went a ridiculous pace, but the track had taken so much water and was holding it pretty well, so it was tight," Baffert said.

Smith could feel he was going fast, "But looking at my horse, he was well within himself and I thought, 'Okay,'" he said. "I took a peek to my side and saw Bolt d'Oro there, and I looked over my shoulder, and there was Good Magic. Those were the horses I thought we had to beat, and they were right with me. So I figured if I was going quicker than I wanted to, so are they. They're laying right on top of me."

Baffert agreed. "The main concerns were Bolt and Good Magic," he said. "If they had been five or six lengths behind us, then I think we would have been a sitting duck out there. But they were right in the fight with us, so I felt pretty good about that."

Up the backstretch nothing changed among the leaders. The pace finally did slow down, with Promises Fulfilled going the first six furlongs (three-quarters of a mile) in 1:11.01. At that point, with a half-mile remaining in the race, Promises Fulfilled hit the proverbial wall. Justify cruised to the lead outside of him on the second turn. Bolt d'Oro was also calling for his check and backed out of it. Smith felt confident as he grabbed the advantage and came out of the turn, straightening away toward the finish line a quarter-mile away.

"He's just a special, special horse," said the rider. "He does things very easily and comfortably. Although we went in :45, I was leaning back on him more than I normally would because Bolt d'Oro came outside and pushed him along a bit. But Justify is so athletic. He gets over the ground so easy and is able to keep running. It takes a lot to try to keep up with him. Sometimes you've got to let a fast horse be fast and let the others try to come and run him down.

"When you get a horse with this kind of talent and a stride like his, it's just about getting into a rhythm. You get them into a nice, happy rhythm, and they're going to run their race. I felt very confident down the backstretch. We put Promises Fulfilled away and I was able to just sit for a little bit, and he took some air in. As soon as I called on him again, he jumped right back into the bridle and was all racehorse. Then it's just a matter of if you can hold off the closers."

Right on cue, Good Magic, who was running in fifth position between horses, left his company behind and was shifted to the outside of Justify by jockey Jose Ortiz. The game colt tried to make a race of it, getting to within a length and a half of the leader.

"That's why I put those long works into him," Baffert said, referring to the six- and seven-furlong workouts he gave Justify after the Santa Anita Derby. "You try to prepare him so that if he does get into a fight, he's ready. I wanted to make sure he's not going to get tired on me; that he's going to keep on."

Watching Justify come off the final turn, Baffert still didn't feel like he was out of the woods. Like Walden, he flashed back to 2012, when his trainee Bodemeister had set fractions freakishly similar to what was unfolding before him. Bodemeister actually opened a three-length lead at the top of the stretch—with Smith in the saddle—and got caught by Gutierrez and I'll Have Another.

"He turned for home and he was still there," Baffert noted of Justify. "But I was thinking back to Bodemeister and I just didn't know. I was wondering if Mike did it to me again. And then all of a sudden someone was coming. Good Magic. Wow, he's a good horse. This is the toughest bunch I've seen in a Derby I've been involved in. There are some really good horses in there."

Besides having to worry about Good Magic, Audible, who had been mired back in 12th place for much of the race, began weaving his way through traffic, cutting outside and then steered back toward the rail by jockey Javier Castellano, and he was passing horses with just about each stride. But Justify, who alone among the 19 other mud-encrusted runners was clean as a dog just back from the groomers, had still more to give.

"When Justify turned for home, I got back all in on him because he still looked strong," said Walden. "It didn't look like he was shortening stride, even though Audible was making a big run. That's a great horse, to run those fractions and not be shortening stride."

"He felt like he wasn't going to let anyone get by him, and that's something I felt in all his races," stated Smith.

Justify ran as a determined champion down the stretch of the Derby, unwavering in his charge to the wire. He increased his advantage to 2½ lengths and steadfastly maintained that margin to the finish line, which he arrived at in 2:04.20. Good Magic held second place by just a head from the fast-charging Audible. Bolt d'Oro faltered to finish 12th; Promises Fulfilled 15th; and Mendelssohn checked in last, being eased by his rider down the stretch.

Justify's win gave Baffert his fifth Kentucky Derby and moved him into second place, one behind Ben Jones, on the all-time Derby victory list for trainers. Jones trained for the powerhouse Calumet Farm outfit in the middle of the 20th century when it dominated racing.

"I knew the last eighth of a mile he was going to win," said Baffert. "And I'm in awe of his performance. That's the best Kentucky Derby–winning performance we've had. Justify just put himself up there with the greats. We knew he was capable of it; he's shown us and we talked about it quietly among ourselves, but I didn't want to say it in public. Hey, I didn't want to jinx myself. We knew we had something really special, but he had to go out and prove it today."

It's a necessity to hold press conferences immediately following major sporting events. Horse racing adheres to this formula, but it has a far different dynamic than team sports, where each squad has a 50/50 chance of victory. In the Kentucky Derby, holding that each horse has a shot to win, there is but a 5 percent chance that a given horse will hit the wire first. Therefore, doubt and low expectations are probably a good idea to stave off bitter disappointment. As for the winners, it is the surest thing in the sport that none of them have their thoughts in order so soon after winning the Kentucky Derby. In the minutes and even hours and days after the race, they drift along in a merry haze not sure what has happened and with a disbelief that they have actually gained racing's ultimate prize. They acknowledge all of this freely, and it is only after they return to their homes and watch the race on replay several dozen times that the result actually sinks in.

Baffert has learned through his 20 years in the spotlight how to be media-savvy. An interview with him typically meanders, with sentences taking sharp turns in the middle to address aspects of a subject that haven't been asked. Part of that is by design. No trainer of horses wants to give too much away, no matter how media-friendly they may be. In this, Baffert takes up the model perfected by the great New York Yankees manager Casey Stengel, whose monologues are legendary for wandering afield and then partially returning to the vicinity of the question at hand. When the reporter's head stopped swimming and he checked his notes, he may or may not have gotten what he'd come for, but he had something.

Baffert began the post-Derby press conference following Justify's victory with a 10-minute monologue that somehow touched on thanking the horse's owners, going back over Justify's race career, the "Apollo Curse," his team back at the barn, his father-in-law, Smith, and the jinx involving the color of Jill's dress. In the midst of it, though, he opened a window not normally seen about what actually goes through a trainer's head in the days before sending out a horse to run in the Kentucky Derby.

"A lot of people come up to you and ask if you're having fun," said Baffert from the press conference podium. "Leading up to the race, I'm not having fun. I'm miserable. When they win, then I start having fun. It's a lot of pressure. When you have a horse like this in the most important race of our life, it's pressure.

"This is a great sport. It's a lot of fun. But it's tough, and there are times you really have to go through it. It's not going to be roses every day, and you have to gut it out. You get that call that your horse is injured or something, and it just rips your soul, I'm telling you. So you have to have that passion. These animals are so beautiful. I get to be around them every day, horses like Justify, McKinzie. And you know, sometimes they will break your heart."

Then he turned the dial: "And to win it with a horse as great as this one is, I mean, not only that, but he's the most beautiful horse, a specimen of a horse. You guys saw him when he walked up there. This guy, he's just special. I mean, he just, he has that presence about him.

"Every day that he goes out to train at Santa Anita, everybody asks, 'Who is that?' And he's the only one I know for sure who it is. It's a great feeling."

As much presence as he has, as good-looking as he is, and as much natural talent and speed as he has been blessed with, Justify's mind as much as anything sets him apart. The way he has handled everything thrown at him, from the travel to the constant crowds to the cameras pointed at him to new surroundings to the rigors of the race itself—and in just his fourth lifetime race to boot—is extraordinary. And Smith, who became, at 52, the second-oldest jockey to win a Kentucky Derby (Bill Shoemaker was 54 when he won the 1986 edition with Ferdinand), appreciated Justify's temperament more than anyone.

"He is so talented," Smith said. "He's unbelievable, and he has the mind to go with it. He can go in :45 and still finish like he did, and that's incredible. Listen, by no means did I think we had it won at the beginning, but after we got away from the gate cleanly, I was like, 'You do it from here.' I just basically stayed out of his way and kept a leg on each side and my mind in the middle. And when I called on him turning for home, he switched over to his right lead and dug back in. They could have gone around the track again, and he wasn't going to let them by.

"He's just an amazing horse. I have never been on a 3-year-old like this."

Filled by Justify's roster of owners, the press-conference podium was nearly as crowded as the Derby starting gate had been. Chairs were lined up on the riser from one wall to the other as the ownership groups represented their winner. WinStar's connections, since they owned majority interest in the colt, took the lead.

"You just feel blessed," Walden said when asked about his thoughts. "We're grateful for the Troutts and the opportunities they provide for us. We have a plaque in our office that says, 'Proverbs 21:31: The horse is made ready for the day of battle but victory rests with the Lord.' That's what we live every day for. The Troutts are believers in Jesus Christ. And we are, too. And it's just great to share that with them. It's not why we won today, because we get beat plenty. But it's just really an opportunity for us as a family to share the blessings that God has given us.

"But you can't do it without good horses. A lot of people out there work really hard and don't have the resources we do. This is a great ownership group. Mr. Teo and the China Horse Club, and SF Bloodstock. They entrusted us and gave us the opportunity to spread out and buy more colts."

Troutt, a quiet man usually content to stay out of the spotlight, certainly has seen racing from all sides, from the modest leaky-roof tracks of Nebraska to the glory of winning the Derby twice at Churchill Downs.

"It's a very special thing," he noted, "and I want to thank all these partners we have. They invest in our stallions and have mares on our farm, and it's just been a blessing to have them. They enable us to go out and buy more horses and that allows us a better shot of winning the Derby.

"When I kept hearing Bob talk about how special this horse was, I got so high because we have had good horses, but never really a great, great horse."

China Horse Club was winning its second huge race on Derby weekend in as many years, Abel Tasman having taken the Kentucky Oaks a year before Justify captured the Derby. If Teo Ah Khing needed quick results in order to impress the Chinese government and people about a potential expansion of Thoroughbred racing in the homeland, he certainly got what he was looking for.

"We set up a five-year plan, to be honest with you," Teo told the media after the Derby. "This is our third year, so we have gone beyond our goals. We have about 16 Chinese members of our group here today, all captains of industry in China. This win today is equivalent to a gold medal in the Olympics for China Horse Club and for the Chinese people regarding Thoroughbred racing.

"So I want to thank America for allowing China Horse Club to set foot here and for the wonderful partners you see here. And I want to echo our brother Elliott that when you are really trusting in the Lord, I think the doors open. It is almost an impossible thing that has happened for us last year in the Kentucky Oaks and this year in the Kentucky Derby."

Teo took a pause from his spiritual statement to throw in a brief commercial for the CHC's racetrack project in Saint Lucia when he introduced the island's prime minister, Allen Chastanet, who knew what to do with the free time.

"We are going to have our first major horse race in Saint Lucia in February, and we look forward to seeing everybody down there," Chastanet said. "And congratulations to Teo. He has big dreams, but he backs up those dreams, and we are here to live those dreams with him."

No representatives of SF Bloodstock were up on the podium. Although it was known by many within the horse industry, a *New York Times* article tying the group's origins to George Soros was still a month from publication, and SF's officers maintain a Greta Garbo–like distance from any publicity.

Jack Wolf, the Louisville native, and Sol Kumin, minor players in Justify at 15 percent, seemed, if not embarrassed, then hesitant to say much in the wake of their victory. Both Wolf and Kumin have many horses which their groups own 100 percent of, and they were quite aware that as great as this moment was, they were supporting players, not the main attraction. Good minority partners put up their money, enjoy whatever good fortune comes their way, and keep quiet.

"You don't want to be a jerk," Kumin said later, privately. "You know it's not your show." Publicly, he thanked his partners in Justify. Months later, Kumin spoke about the effect that winning the Derby has on day-to-day life.

"As far as getting into this sport, the Derby is the big win," he said. "Winning races like the Kentucky Oaks and the Travers is just as hard to do, but to your friends outside racing—I now get introduced as, 'This is my friend Sol, who won the Kentucky Derby.'

"When it hits you is later the night of the race. It's certainly one of the things I thought would be amazing to do when I got into the sport a few years ago. You can't believe it actually happened. It's a bucket-list item. Then you try to get back to your life, but it becomes all-consuming. You can't concentrate on work because the Preakness is coming right up, and you're wondering if the horse can win the next leg."

Wolf summed it up when he said, "We're tickled to death to be along for the ride, and we thank Elliott, Mr. Troutt, and Mr. Teo for letting us get on the bandwagon."

When John Asher asked Smith the secret to his success at his relatively advanced age, the rider noted, "Keep riding horses like this; they'll keep you around a long time. They do all the work for you. When Bob told me about him back in California, I've been losing sleep ever since, but in a good way. I've been so excited just dreaming about this horse.

"What happened during the race is what I've been daydreaming about all afternoon. I knew he was capable of this. I got him out of the gate, and I figured the rest was up to him. Bob and his crew already did their part. And he's just an amazing horse.

"Right now, I'm more relieved than anything. Later on, I'll start getting excited as it hits me. I'm on a horse where it looks like anything can be possible."

The final question as these press conferences end is always directed at the trainer, asking what time they will be at the barn the following morning for an update on the condition of the race winner. Baffert gave another rambling answer, admitting he was in the middle of an out-of-body experience. Somewhere during this soliloquy, he mentioned he would be flying out the following day and planned to be at the barn early in the AM to check on the horse.

He wound up wishing he'd flown back to California without seeing Justify the next morning.

13

BRUISED, FOGGED IN, AND STILL UNBEATEN

IMMEDIATELY AFTER THE DERBY PRESS CONFERENCE, BAFFERT returned to the barn to check on Justify, who had cooled out, eaten up, and looked good, allowing the trainer to head to a Derby party that evening. Early the following morning Baffert called his chief assistant Barnes, who was already at the barn and reported that Justify looked perfect. It is a big relief getting through the first night after a race without incident, making sure the horse gets into his feed, hasn't spiked a fever, or incurred an injury that won't show itself until the following day.

Before heading to the airport and his flight back west, Baffert came to the barn to look Justify over. The horse gave him all the right signals. Baffert walked Justify through his barn for several laps as members of the media assembled, waiting to talk to the trainer and perhaps catch a glimpse of the colt as well. Just outside the barn, Churchill Downs had put down new gravel that had jagged edges to it. Baffert's first thought was not to bring Justify out, but he also was proud of his horse and a part of him wanted to show him off. A couple of mats were placed over the gravel, and so Baffert brought Justify out to be admired.

As photographers and videographers shot the chestnut, all initially seemed fine. Then Justify's right rear foot hit the mat and immediately shot up into the air. Baffert, thinking the horse was in great shape, was blindsided as the Derby winner all of a sudden was favoring the leg, a red flag that seemed to threaten the horse's chances going forward.

"He'd had a spot in the same area where he bruised his heel after his second race, which was in the mud at Santa Anita," said Baffert. "For the Santa Anita Derby, we took a quarter of his shoe off where it was hitting the bruised area. For the Kentucky Derby, we put a full shoe back on him. And then, all of a sudden, when he walked out on the gravel that morning, he woke up that area and gave on it, and the video caught him. It was the same heel he'd had a problem in before, so we wanted to get on it and soak it right away and get after it. So we cut a quarter of his shoe off to be able to work on it and get the heat out of it so it didn't get worse."

Baffert decided to go ahead and leave town despite the issue, believing it wouldn't turn into anything major. Despite the condition being minor in the trainer's mind, the media reaction was altogether different, and the day-after Derby stories were dominated by the news of Justify having become lame.

"To the public, it was a big deal," said Walden. "But if you were in the know, in the trenches, you weren't worried about it."

By the time Baffert was preparing to board his flight, his cell was blowing up from reporters calling and looking for comment. He turned off the phone. A farrier (blacksmith) was brought in to take a look at Justify's heel. He applied a patch to the area to reinforce it, make it stronger, and prevent the formation of a quarter crack, a vertical split in the wall of the hoof.

Baffert said that by the next day, the heel was "already 100 percent better." But he still had to deal with outside forces, such as PETA, the animal-rights organization that has called for a ban on horse racing and which has attempted sting operations, including taking secret video and then doctoring it through editing in an attempt to discredit the sport. It sent a letter to the Kentucky

Horse Racing Commission, which normally would have had nothing to do with a horse having a heel bruise following a race.

"Commission members came out to see the horse, and my vet told them how we had X-rayed the foot and took super-precautions to make sure what the injury was," said Baffert. "We jogged the horse for them so they could see everything was fine and kill the PETA story. It was a 72-hour fiasco, and that was that. We told them everything and had total transparency.

"You have the Derby winner and I understand all eyes are on us, but I was angry at myself for having brought him out of the barn the morning after the race."

With just two weeks between the Kentucky Derby and the Preakness, the second leg of the Triple Crown that is run at Pimlico Race Course in Baltimore, Baffert had no plans to give Justify a timed workout anyway, so the foot bruise had little effect on his training regimen. After as taxing a race as the Derby, horses wouldn't normally go back to the racetrack for a morning jog or gallop for three or four days, and would be walked around the shedrow during that time.

It is an amazing achievement that previous to Justify, all four of Baffert's Kentucky Derby winners—Silver Charm, Real Quiet, War Emblem, and American Pharoah—continued on to win the Preakness as well. In addition, Point Given, who looked like a lock to win the 2001 Kentucky Derby but ran a mystifyingly flat race that day; and Lookin At Lucky, who drew the dreaded number 1 post position in the Derby and had little chance in the race, had also come back and won the Preakness. Although the first three of the four Baffert horses who went for the Triple Crown came up short in the Belmont Stakes, Point Given and American Pharoah dominated the Belmont. With Justify's Derby victory, Baffert had earned his 13th win in Triple Crown races, leaving him one behind the leading mark of 14 held by D. Wayne Lukas.

Lukas wasn't going to let Baffert continue on the Triple Crown trail without a fight, however. Bravazo, bumped at the start of the Derby, raced in mid-pack most of the way before making headway down the stretch. He finished with a flourish to wind up sixth at 66-1, and Lukas had no hesitation about bringing him right back to try the Preakness.

Baffert kept Justify at Churchill Downs for a week and a half after the Derby. The colt recovered fully from his bruise and was galloping well in Kentucky. Meanwhile, in Baltimore, it never stopped raining in the week before the Preakness. If Derby Day seemed to have an issue with Mother Nature, Preakness week was right there with it. Including the 2018 edition, three of the last four Preaknesses were run over sloppy racetracks.

On the Wednesday before the Preakness, Baffert flew to Baltimore, arriving before Justify's flight was scheduled to get in from Louisville. Unlike at the Derby or Belmont Stakes, where the horses are spread out in various barns throughout the backstretch area, at Pimlico all the Preakness horses are housed together under one roof, known as the stakes barn. That situation makes it possible for reporters to cover the horses without expending a lot of shoe leather, and also makes it easy for trainers to size up their competition leading up to the race.

When Baffert arrived at the stakes barn May 16 to wait for Justify to get in from the airport, he found a familiar figure sitting outside: Wayne Lukas.

"He sits at that corner of the barn and watches everything," said Baffert. "The great horsemen, they don't let on, but I pushed him about how it looked so far, and he said, 'Don't worry about those other ones. I've been watching them here.' He asked how my horse was doing, and I said, 'Great,' and a few minutes later here comes the van. I bring him off the van and I'm walking him around the barn, and I stop the horse right in front of Wayne. I said, 'What do you think?' And Wayne is staring at him and just goes, 'Wow.'

"I said, 'Wayne, is it like *Jaws* when the guy sees the shark for the first time and says, 'We're going to need a bigger boat?' And he nodded and said, 'Yeah, but I think I can run second to you.'

"Wayne is such a competitive guy, and he was excited about his horse. He never wavers. You'll never see him raise the white flag. He's just that way. He's never gonna give up. And that tells you how good Justify looked."

Well before the Preakness, Baffert and Lukas had a long and complicated history with one another. Lukas, 18 years Baffert's senior, was a former high school teacher and basketball coach in his native Wisconsin before he set out to train Quarter Horses in 1968. He became the dominant trainer in the sport, and made a huge impression on Baffert, then a high school student, when Lukas would bring his horses in for big races in Arizona.

"He was the king," Baffert wrote in his autobiography. "I really liked his style. I saw him for the first time in Sonoita, Arizona, and when he showed up, he just took over. It was like Barnum and Bailey rolling into town. He was a showman to the max, and I really liked that."

After Baffert graduated high school, he raised the nerve to call up Lukas and ask him for a job galloping horses. Instead of turning him down flat, Lukas built Baffert up, telling him he'd be perfect for his operation, but that he'd just hired someone a few days before. It was likely the showman in Lukas coming through, but probably for the best, as well.

"Thank god he didn't hire me," Baffert said recently with tongue in cheek. "I don't know how long I would have lasted. He gets up too early in the morning, and I'd have had to listen to all his stories."

Lukas' influence on Baffert can't be discounted, however. Lukas left Quarter Horses after 10 years to move on to Thoroughbreds, a move mirrored by Baffert. And when Baffert was stuck in the middle training both breeds at once, it was Lukas who told him to get out of the Quarter Horses and concentrate on the Thoroughbreds.

Fate continually seemed to bring the two of them together. Baffert suffered that cruel nose defeat to Lukas in the 1996 Kentucky Derby. And while Baffert was establishing his relationship with owner Bob Lewis, Lukas also wooed the deep-pocketed beer distributor, and was a far better and more experienced salesman who pitched Lewis on a three-year plan while Baffert was struggling to find one horse to buy for the owner at auctions.

Eventually, Baffert worked his way up to equivalent status with Lukas in Lewis' orbit, the product of having sold him on Silver Charm and winning the 1997 Kentucky Derby and Preakness for Lewis with the colt. Lukas, meanwhile, trained the multiple champion and eventual Hall of Fame filly Serena's Song for Lewis, and so the horse sales became a three-ring circus among the men, with Baffert and Lukas both jockeying to buy top prospects for Lewis, one seated at Lewis' side and the other leaning over in his ear from a row behind.

Bloodstock agent John Moynihan, whom Lewis had plucked from obscurity and hired to buy and sell horses for him, had a front-row seat for the competition between the two trainers.

"Wayne was at the pinnacle of his profession in the mid-'90s and Bob was coming up and doing extremely well, and Bob Lewis was really the primary client of both of them," noted Moynihan. "Obviously, there are just a limited number of select individuals at these sales that you really love, and when Mr. Lewis would buy these horses, you'd have both Wayne and Bob giving him advice, and sometimes the advice would be on the same horse, and then

Mr. Lewis and [his wife] Beverly would have to decide which trainer would get the horse.

"Both Wayne and Bob were extremely competitive. And as upset as one of them would be not getting a certain horse, the irony was sometimes the consolation horse one of them got instead was the one that took them to the Promised Land."

Moynihan and Lewis had bought an expensive weanling one year who would be named Exploit. After failing to resell him as a yearling, Lewis put Exploit into training and gave him to Baffert. Exploit became a graded stakes winner but was injured before the Triple Crown races, and sold as a stallion prospect for $12 million. Meanwhile, the horse Bob Lewis gave to Lukas to assuage his missing out on Exploit would become Charismatic, whom Lukas trained to victory in the 1999 Kentucky Derby and Preakness for Lewis.

"They got upset," Moynihan said of the two trainers. "Bob was probably better at letting things roll off his back a little easier than Wayne, but a week later, you'd never know anything had happened. Bob Lewis would put his foot down and one of them would get mad, but everything was good. It was just their competitive nature."

The one rift that left the two trainers at odds for a time occurred because of a newspaper article written by a Louisville reporter Derby week of 1996. Baffert had Cavonnier in the race, and Lukas had five runners in the field. The reporter asked Baffert what he thought about the discrepancy.

"I said the business was driven by ego and that all these owners want to be in the Derby," Baffert said. "Only the reporter wrote it like I was saying it was Wayne's ego that led him to running the five horses. So I'm at the track Derby Day and Wayne comes up to me and angrily confronts me about why I said those things in the paper. I hadn't read the paper and didn't know what he was talking about, so I said, 'What do you mean, that I said your cowboy hat looks like it got caught in an elevator?' Because I *had* said that. And he said, 'No, that I entered those horses because of my ego.' I told him I didn't say that.

"I think reporters were trying to knock him down. I've since been through that; a lot of us have been through that. Wayne was always my idol. Some of these guys saw an opening to sort of get us, and we became collateral damage of those stories. So that caused a thing between us for a couple of years. I was never upset at him, and I didn't want him to be mad at me. I've known him forever and have always had the most respect for him, and I never wanted him to think I'd lost that respect.

"It was a bad deal there, and a conflict for a little bit, but we got through it and got together again, and it's all good. He's one of the greatest trainers and greatest people. What he's done is amazing, and he's still a sharp horseman."

Lukas downplayed any rift between himself and Baffert. "First of all, Bob and I were friends long before Bob Lewis," he said. "And our friendship led to him moving over to Thoroughbreds. But when we were both training for Bob [Lewis] and we were both in all the major races, the media made it out like we were big rivals. At no time during that whole stretch did our friendship suffer. When those articles came out about how we were knocking heads, we were going out to dinner together.

"I feel good that our friendship led to his getting into the Thoroughbred business with both feet, and the fact I had some influence on that makes me feel good because he is an exceptional horse trainer. Don't underestimate him. He knows where to get the good horses, and he sure knows what to do with them."

Lukas also knew what he was up against going into the Preakness. Three years earlier at the Kentucky Derby, he had watched American Pharoah, whose abnormally small tail is about a third the size of an average one, train. Asked to assess that Derby field at the time, Lukas famously said, "That horse with the short tail has them all over a barrel."

Lukas said he'd had a déjà vu experience when he watched Justify train up to the 2018 Kentucky Derby. "I felt even more so when I saw him," said Lukas. "He's a great physical specimen, with a conformation form that I like. I had talked with Bob early on and he said the horse was exceptional, but he didn't know if he could get him ready in time. So this is a remarkable training job. Let's give the horse credit; he's the best horse here. But having said that, not everyone could have done what Bob Baffert did with him."

Justify looked bright while galloping through the muck at Pimlico the couple of days he was there before the Preakness. He had no way of knowing, of course, that the day before the race, an agreement was reached that would change where he would live his life following his race career.

It was always assumed that being a stallion operation, his majority owner WinStar Farm would be anxious to add Justify to its stallion ranks once the colt was retired from racehorse duty. Major farms around Kentucky routinely enter bidding wars to obtain prospects such as Justify, whose pedigree, looks, and race record made him as desirable as any potential sire to have come down the pike in years. And WinStar officials repeatedly had said they go to yearling sales specifically to try and buy colts who will prove out as racehorses and then subsequently be retired to the farm as a stallion. Justify was the poster boy for such a plan coming to fruition.

As the crow flies, Ashford Stud near Versailles, Kentucky, sits no more than a couple of miles from WinStar. Ashford is the American satellite of the worldwide Coolmore operation, which began in Ireland and has branched out to America and Australia. Coolmore by and large dominates stakes races in Europe through its stable at Ballydoyle, headed by trainer Aidan O'Brien. Its superiority is fueled by the progeny of top stallions it has nurtured, namely Danehill, Sadler's Wells, and Galileo.

From a small farm and then training operation established just after World War II, Coolmore in Ireland currently stretches more than 7,000 acres, built up by John Magnier, the son-in-law of legendary Irish trainer Vincent O'Brien. Magnier has made a fortune with several investments, and once owned 30 percent of the Manchester United football (soccer) team. His worth is estimated to be around $4-$5 billion.

Ashford in Kentucky came to prominence some 30 years before Justify's arrival. In some combination of Magnier and partners such as Michael Tabor and Derrick Smith, Coolmore has won dozens of North American graded stakes races, including the Kentucky Derby and Belmont Stakes in 1995 (under Tabor's name) with Thunder Gulch, who subsequently stood at stud at Ashford. For the past 20 years, Ashford has competed for top stallions with the other headline farms in the Bluegrass Region. Scat Daddy, the sire of Justify, was on his way to star status in the Ashford stallion barn when he died unexpectedly in 2015 at age 11. He had been the leading freshman sire of 2011 and had already sired an excellent total of 69 stakes winners at the time of his death.

While Ashford boasts a solid stallion roster, as of May of 2018, it lacked a true superstar at stud. American Pharoah calls Ashford home, and looks to have every chance to become a top— and perhaps superstar—sire. His first crop of sons and daughters are yearlings of 2018, and at that September's yearling auction at Keeneland, his progeny proved most popular, averaging more than $400,000 and going for as high as $2.2 million, by far leading his class. But none of his progeny will hit the racetrack until mid-2019, so it is too soon to know just how prepotent he might be. Ashford's Uncle Mo has established himself as a top sire just below superstar status, but certainly there is always the desire to add to a stallion roster.

The Thoroughbred industry is a relatively small universe, and rumors spread throughout it like the children's game of Post Office, where whispers are passed along from one to another in a wave. It was shocking when those whispers in the days following the Preakness detailed a deal had been reached for the post-racing-career sale of Justify by WinStar (and partners) to Ashford, meaning Ashford would own the colt for breeding purposes. The story received denials from the two principal parties, but that was chalked up to the fact that nothing would become "official" until September of 2018 because of tax purposes. Knowledgeable sources throughout the industry confirmed that the deal had in fact been struck on Preakness Eve. The terms were believed to be a $60 million base payment from Ashford to WinStar and its partners, with "kickers" in the deal escalating that amount to between $75-$85 million should Justify successfully complete the Triple Crown.

Almost on cue, the deal was officially announced in September of 2018.

AS PREAKNESS DAY DAWNED, eight runners prepared to do battle. Besides Justify, the Kentucky Derby runner-up Good Magic was readying to build on that strong effort. Lukas' Bravazo was in, as was Derby eighth-place finisher Lone Sailor. Lukas had another contender in Sporting Chance; Tenfold, who hadn't made it into the Derby field, showed up in the Preakness; and a speedy horse named Quip, owned by WinStar, SF, and China Horse Club, also was entered, interesting because he potentially could push Justify on the lead.

Whereas Thoroughbreds in eras past routinely raced every week, and even more frequently than that sometimes, now the two-week break between the Kentucky Derby and Preakness represents the shortest turnaround that top racehorses are likely to face in their careers. There is always concern about the closeness of those races not leaving enough recovery time, particularly for the Derby winner attempting to advance along the Triple Crown trail. Most horsemen today will skip the Preakness if their horses run unsuccessfully in the Derby because the time between those races is just too short for their comfort. And the sloppy condition of the Pimlico racing surface wouldn't have enticed any of them to change their mind during this week.

The connections of the Derby winner have no real choice but to run back in the Preakness, and it had been 33 years since the last Derby winner didn't try the Preakness for reason other than injury. In 1985, the owner of Derby winner Spend A Buck, Dennis Diaz, elected to skip the Preakness in favor of the Jersey Derby, in a successful attempt to cash in on a $2 million bonus Spend A Buck earned by winning both derbies plus two previous races in the Garden State.

Justify, after having recovered from his foot bruise, was giving his connections little reason to be hesitant about the quick turnaround.

"I would have been more concerned if he hadn't run on a sloppy track twice before, and run well over them," Walden noted. "He was training well. When we had [2010 Derby winner] Super Saver, he wasn't in his feed tub after the Derby and he wasn't showing good energy. Justify had a different constitution. I didn't feel like he'd get beat that day."

Breeder John Gunther repaired back to his farm in Alberta, Canada, after the Derby, taking himself physically off the Triple Crown trail for one race. Even though he'd bred two of the

Derby starters, Churchill Downs would not sell him a box for the day, which added to the lack of a good experience he'd had in Louisville that week.

"At the post position draw they wouldn't let Tanya and me in the room," he said. "We went in anyway and told them we weren't leaving, and they called security. It was unbelievable. Nothing was easy."

For the Preakness Gunther booked a large room with multiple TV monitors at the Derby Bar & Grill near his farm outside Vancouver, a place where he and his guests could wager and watch the races. "We had a great time," he said. "It was fantastic. I was ordering the champagne before the race. I knew he'd win that one."

Once again, weather was going to play a factor, as the incessant rain that had pelted Baltimore all week continued through the morning of the race.

The weather was certainly affecting the outlook of Larry Collmus, a Baltimore native who was preparing to announce the races on NBC that day. Collmus, 51, had been the track announcer at various venues along the East Coast when he was selected in 2011 to succeed the legendary Tom Durkin as the voice of the Triple Crown races and Breeders' Cup on NBC. Four years later, Collmus would also replace the retiring Durkin at the microphone of the prestigious New York Racing Association tracks—Belmont Park, Saratoga, and Aqueduct.

In his first year at NYRA, Collmus got to call a Triple Crown winner in American Pharoah, something that had eluded Durkin during his 27-year tenure at NBC and 25 years at NYRA. In preparation for calling the Kentucky Derby each year, Collmus begins months in advance by watching prep races and familiarizing himself with probable contenders. He makes flashcards of the owners' silks that will be carried by the Derby runners, memorizing them well before Derby Day so that there are no slipups during the year's most crucial two minutes. He also takes note of the horses' color and any distinguishing characteristics.

"By the time they come onto the track for the Derby, you want those 20 horses to be your best friends and know them as well as you can," Collmus said. "The weather is another reason why I do that, because there's a good chance they will have mud all over their silks, so you want to know any markings they have. I've called eight Kentucky Derbys, and it seems like it rains every year. You have to be that much more prepared."

With only eight horses to deal with in the Preakness, Collmus should have had an easier preparation. That was not the case, however. A week before the race, he fielded a phone call from NBC producer Rob Hyland telling him of a potential problem at Pimlico. In scouting the location, Hyland discovered that between hospitality tents set up in the infield for corporate sponsors and a giant concert stage that was erected for musical entertainment, there was going to be a one-eighth-mile blind spot where Collmus would not be able to see the racetrack's backstretch.

"Normally I have two monitors up in the booth that are off to the side that I use only to keep an eye on the NBC show," said Collmus. "I never use them to call the races. But Rob said they were going to give me two high-definition monitors so I could use them for that portion of the race when the track would be obscured from my view.

"At 1:00 there was a meteorologist from a local TV station up on the roof near me doing a live report. He said the rain should be ending in the next 30 minutes and it would be dry the rest of the day. But he didn't say anything about fog. Didn't mention that. I had no idea it was coming, and it started to get worse and worse and worse.

"When you call a race in the fog, you hope it's so bad that you can't see anything, because at that point everyone knows it's impossible, and you can have fun with it; mess around and have a good time. But not if it's a Triple Crown race. You have to do what you can do.

"During a commercial break right before the race, they showed me the various camera shots they had so I'd have an idea what I was in for. Not only couldn't I see the starting gate up the stretch, I couldn't see the sixteenth pole right in front of me. They decided at the last minute to send a cameraman down next to the starting gate, and so he was able to grab the start of the race. For the most part they had enough coverage where I wasn't completely gone; I could get through it okay. But thank goodness for those concert stages because it turned out I called 90 percent of the race off those two monitors."

Justify left from post position 7 once again, Good Magic was in the number 5 gate, and Quip had the rail.

"The plan was to stay clean," said Baffert. "Get out of there and go up toward the front. I didn't have any problem with Quip going to the lead, as long as he was going fast enough. We thought it would be fine to follow someone around there like we did in the Derby."

Justify broke alertly under Smith and set out for the lead. However, there were two trails across his path as he approached the finish line for the first time—tracks left by officials and photographers who had walked across the sloppy track to get to positions inside the inner rail. It is not uncommon for horses who see tracks or shadows across the racetrack to jump them, literally breaking their stride to soar over the differences they perceive on the surface. Justify jumped tracks twice as he came by the grandstand, losing his rhythm and allowing the horse inside him to catch up.

That horse, however, wasn't Quip. It was Good Magic, who was flying up inside Justify and just a head in back of the Derby winner. Those were not the instructions given by trainer Brown to his rider Jose Ortiz. Brown believed it was going to be Diamond King, one of the longest shots on the board, who was going to sprint from the gate and keep Justify company early, and Brown wanted Good Magic tucked in behind the early pace so he could make a late run if the tempo was too quick.

If you want to hear God laugh…

One of the talents exhibited by the great jockeys is the ability to adjust. If Plan A isn't coming to fruition, go to Plan B, or Plan C. Mike Smith knew what was at stake here.

"The Preakness to me was more nerve-wracking than the other two Triple Crown races," he stated. "We'd already won the Derby, and I felt if we could pull this one off, I really believed the Belmont would be the track he'd like best. It has those big old sweeping wide turns and he's a big old powerful-striding horse, and those are the kind that usually get over that track. He reminded me of Easy Goer [the 1989 Belmont winner who previously lost the Derby and Preakness to Sunday Silence], a big, powerful horse who got hindered by the tight turns a little bit, but at the Belmont I could let him run around those big turns.

"I was going to take the lead, but Justify jumped the tracks, and then he did it a second time and allowed Good Magic to come up to our inside. I thought, 'Okay, fine, this is the horse to beat, and we're head-to-head. I'll just get away from him a little bit.' I figured it would be a two-horse race unless someone else ran the race of their life."

Justify, as was his wont throughout his career, wouldn't let Good Magic in front of him, but the two raced nose-and-nose for the entire length of the backstretch. This time, the fractions were reasonable: the first quarter-mile in :23.11, half-mile in :47.19, and three-quarters in 1:11.42. Bravazo stayed outside of Justify and two lengths in back of the leading pair. Down the backstretch, and indiscernible through the fog, Ortiz and Good Magic were trying to push Justify out wider on the track.

"Good Magic took it to him and tried to bully him a little bit, which I totally understand," said Smith. "That's race-riding. They weren't doing anything that was hurting anybody, just trying to discourage him a little bit by drifting him out. But he was handling it so well, it was fine with me if we just went a little wider."

The horses moved into the final turn and out of sight, obscured by the thick blanket of fog. Going into the curve, Justify and Good Magic were still in front of the field.

"There was a point on the far turn where they were completely covered in fog for an eighth of a mile," Collmus said. "I bided my time at that juncture and talked about the three-quarter fraction until they emerged. When they came out of the fog for the home straight, the weird thing was we had a camera from behind them and it looked like Justify had pulled away by a length and a half. But when we came back to the pan shot [from the side], Good Magic is still glued to him, and I was like, 'What the hell happened? I thought he was gone.' Then I saw Bravazo and Tenfold coming, and once they all emerged from the fog in the stretch, they got to the wire awful quick. I was calling it from the monitor through to the end."

Going a little wide is one thing, but back on the turn, Smith didn't want to get pushed 10 paths off the rail, so he hit the accelerator. "I got after him a little bit from the quarter pole to the eighth pole just to get his big body moving forward," Smith said. "He was moving good, but I was conscious about not wanting to squeeze the lemon any more than I had to. He had already run pretty fast in the Derby, and I thought if I could just win this race without gutting him, we'd be in good shape going into the Belmont. So I let him idle from inside the eighth pole to the wire."

Coming out of the fog, the first sight seen by viewers was two big chestnut colts, each with a broad white blaze running down their face, engaged in equine combat. Good Magic was still right there to Justify's inside. Smith gave Justify three left-handed urgings to pick it up, and he took a short lead on Good Magic. But now Bravazo and Tenfold were moving boldly in tandem on the outside. Bravazo made up four lengths on Justify from the top of the stretch until the wire, closing the gap late with every stride, and Tenfold was right with him.

Smith did put his stick away and hand-rode Justify inside the sixteenth pole. But the jockey's explanation aside, what the world saw was Justify not being able to pull away from Good Magic, while losing ground to the two pursuers on the outside. And that perception was going to have a big impact on the next three weeks leading up to the Belmont Stakes.

"Bravazo ran a heck of a race," Smith noted. "I didn't see him at first, but I saw him soon enough to know we were going to be fine. We were close to the wire and I knew we had him."

Justify hit the wire a half-length in front of Bravazo in 1:55.93. Tenfold was just a neck in back of Bravazo in third, and Good Magic a neck farther behind Tenfold in fourth. Visually, it looked like Justify had just held on for all he was worth. That was certainly Baffert's fear as he had one eye on the Preakness and the other on the Belmont Stakes three weeks down the road.

"I'm watching the race on this tiny, 12-inch TV monitor and I'm thinking, 'Wow, he won, but that didn't look like a Triple Crown horse right there,'" Baffert said. "I thought when he got away from Good Magic in the fog, that he was going to be five lengths in front, and that we were going to be pounding our chests and crossing the track to the winner's circle like this is going to be the next big horse.

"So I walked up to Mike when he brought the horse back and said, 'Great win, but are we done? Are we empty?'"

Smith talked Baffert back from the ledge as Justify and his trainer walked toward the Preakness winner's circle across the turf course.

"What people couldn't see is that galloping out past the wire, once Bravazo got right next to him, Justify jumped into the bridle and really galloped out strong," Smith said. "He wasn't going to let him pass. Bob really couldn't see much during the race, so I told him that Justify jumped the tracks, that they really took it to him, and that I really didn't ask him to pick it up coming down the stretch. I told him we were fine. He said, 'Really?' And I said, 'Yeah.'"

"Talking to Mike made me feel like we're good," Baffert said. "So I go, 'All riiight. Okay. We're back.' So I went to the barn and waited for my horse and he came back and looked good and cooled out right away and looked bright. Then I went to see Wayne and told him he put a scare into me. Wayne was pumped up that his horse ran so well. I think it put a lot of pep in his step, like 'Don't forget about ol' Wayne.'"

The two men were now tied with 14 victories apiece in Triple Crown races. Both Justify and Bravazo were being pointed to the Belmont Stakes, and that competitive spirit still burned brightly in Lukas.

"I had the best chance to beat him and let him off the hook," Lukas said about Justify's Preakness. "Justify got first run off the turn and we were going to need some racing luck to beat him, because he was the best horse. We needed to move when he did coming around that turn, and we ended up moving a little bit later. We were flying at the end but we ran out of real estate. I thought it was Bravazo's best race of the year. We ran our best and still came up second. That's racing."

Lukas wasn't the only trainer going through "what if" progressions after the race. Brown, who'd seen his best-laid plans fly out the window soon after the Preakness gates opened, was left to wonder what could have been if his strategy to have Good Magic lay off the pace been executed. Several months later, he looked back at the race with perspective.

"I don't want to speculate or take anything away from Justify," he said. "It's important for people to understand that I am well aware of the fact Justify was a better racehorse than Good Magic. I don't dispute that. In fact, I'm sure of it, and that's not to take anything away from Good Magic, who was the second-best horse in his crop.

"That said, the best horse doesn't always win. And if there was any race in his career where Justify was vulnerable, it was the Preakness. He came in nursing some kind of bruise that had been patched; he missed some training. I felt like if we were able to get to his outside early, we would have had a better chance of winning. I will never say that we *would* have beaten him.

"But Justify drew outside of us and that was important. Good Magic didn't have the best trip. But you know what? They both came back in two weeks and Justify sucked it up and overcame a lot of adversity to stay undefeated, and for that I have additional admiration for the horse because I know that was hard to do. And I know how much pressure and concentration it took for Bob and his team to do that.

"I've been in those situations—not with a Triple Crown on the line—but in big races where things are not perfect because of different ailments, and you need to use your expertise and get the right people to work on those issues. You have to be able to call the right audibles with these horses, and it starts at the top. Bob made all the right moves."

As Justify hit the wire first, a large exhale was coming from a hospitality tent set up inside the track near the finish line. There, New York Racing Association senior vice president of racing operations Martin Panza had been rooting for the Derby winner to score again and keep the hope of a Triple Crown alive.

At Belmont Park three weeks hence, a potential Triple Crown meant about 30,000 more people coming through the gates. It also meant that somewhere between $30 million and $50 million more would be wagered on the Belmont Stakes–day races worldwide.

"At the end I saw the Lukas horse coming and it was like, 'Uh-oh,'" Panza said. "Justify kept doing enough to win, though. He wasn't as flashy as American Pharoah, but he kept getting it done."

Humberto Gomez, Justify's exercise rider in the mornings, was the person in charge of bringing Justify his evening meal after the Preakness.

"A lot of horses, when they run a tough race, they don't eat that night or even the next day," Gomez said. "Justify, he never missed a meal. He ate everything. After the Preakness, when he was still warm, he was asking for his feed. When he saw me carrying it, he went crazy. And that's a really good sign."

Early on the morning after the Preakness, Baffert rolled up to the Pimlico stakes barn and got out of his car to go look at his horse. Spirits high, the old jokester emerged in him as he turned toward the media.

"Is there any gravel I can walk my horse on?" Baffert asked.

A couple of hours later, Justify was on a van to the airport and a flight back to Kentucky and Baffert's barn at Churchill Downs, and Baffert was on a jet west to California, two-thirds of racing's greatest prize safely tucked away in his jeans.

14

THE PILOT

IT WAS ONLY FITTING THAT BOB BAFFERT HAD TURNED TO THE counsel of Mike Smith to assess Justify in the moments after the Preakness, and certainly no accident, since the trainer had handpicked Smith to ride this particular horse knowing what a tight spot they all would be in from March hopefully through the Triple Crown series.

Trainers love jockeys who can dismount after a race and tell them exactly how the horse performed, what he likes and doesn't like, and what he might need to improve going forward. This can entail a change of equipment, such as a different bit, blinkers, or shoes; different training regimens; race strategies; or whether a horse is likely to prefer turf or dirt, or shorter or longer distances. A knowledgeable jockey is like having another trainer on track, one who can feel the athlete while he is in action.

At 52, Smith is in a unique position. He has outlasted virtually every one of his generational peers, and his production over the past 15 years allows him to ride only the horses he wants to ride. While other jockeys have their agents hustling to find them six or seven mounts a day, Smith is frequently named on just a horse or two per racing card. He is not financially dependent on quantity of mounts, and his experience and communications skills put him in high demand at his base in California, from where he will also travel the country to partner on top horses competing in stakes action.

Smith is easygoing, and his high-pitched voice grows excited when he discusses the great horses with whom he has partnered. Watching him walk through a paddock before or after a race, you marvel at his patience as he is constantly besieged by fans looking for an autograph, or to take a selfie, or to remember a favorite ride or horse. He is unfailingly polite, though the demands on his time must get exhausting. He knows the attention is all good news, though, and frequently describes himself as being blessed.

He is today so synonymous with riding the best horses in the top races that he is known as "Big Money Mike," the guy you want on your horse when the chips are down and the stakes are highest. Mike Pegram, who never heard a punch line he didn't like, reaped the benefits of Smith's prowess on his McKinzie in 2017 and 2018. Pointing out Smith's selectivity, Pegram affectionately refers to the rider as "By Appointment Only."

Smith wasn't always assigned this lofty status, however. Today it is the product not only of Smith's natural ability, his smarts, and his drive to stay in top shape by being a gym rat, but also his having endured a dark period in his career when he wasn't at all in demand, and the work he had to put in to claw his way back into good graces.

Smith was born to ride horses. He began life in Roswell, New Mexico, the UFO capital of the U.S., and by the age of three or four he was legged up on horses by his family. His father, George Smith, was a jockey, and his uncle, Thomas Vallejos, spent time with the youngster teaching him how to ride. Smith's early career parallels Baffert's. At 11, Smith was riding Quarter Horses on the bush-track circuit around New Mexico, and at the tender age of 14, he dropped out of school to gallop horses as an exercise rider at racetracks throughout the Southwest. As soon as he was old enough at 16 to get his license to ride races, he collected his first Thoroughbred victory at Santa Fe Downs.

"Knowing how to handle a horse came to me at a very young age. I had a gift of knowing what a horse likes and dislikes," allowed Smith. "But everything in New Mexico was speed, speed, speed. I had to learn how to ride in a race, because when you get to the bigger leagues, you find out that patience plays a large role in this game. You have to watch other riders to pick up things like pace, being patient, and other little tactics."

Smith honed his craft at Sunland Park in El Paso, but he knew that in order to improve, he had to hit the road for bigger pastures and greater challenges. Fortunately, he had a close-knit family that was willing to sacrifice to help him achieve his dream. Smith's grandfather, who owned a tavern near Sunland Park, was getting ready to retire, and he sold the business in order to be able to buy a home in Hot Springs, Arkansas, near Oaklawn Park, when Smith moved his tack there in the early 1980s.

"I was scared," Smith said about trying the more competitive racetrack. "I wasn't leaving town unless my grandparents came with me."

When Smith began splitting time between Oaklawn Park and Ak-Sar-Ben in Nebraska, his grandparents travelled back and forth with him.

"They were my main support," he stated.

"Mike was young and had never been away from home," remembered his aunt, Elizabeth Brockmann. "He was a special kid, and Dad wanted to be there for him. Mike was always polite, well-mannered, and has a lot of charisma. And he always wanted to ride horses."

At Oaklawn, Smith began learning some of those "little tactics" by being around riders such as Pat Day, Larry Snyder, and John Lively, and wound up marrying Lively's daughter Patrice.

The life of a young jockey can be nomadic, and Smith rode the circuit from Oaklawn and Nebraska up to Hawthorne Race Course outside Chicago, Canterbury Downs in Minnesota, and Churchill Downs. He started riding some horses for trainer Shug McGaughey at Oaklawn and partnered with the McGaughey-trained Pine Circle to finish sixth in the 1984 Kentucky Derby, his first crack at the Run for the Roses.

By the end of the decade, Smith had gained confidence as a rider and as a man, and he made the decision to move to New York and ride there, on the toughest but most lucrative circuit in the country. And against the most talented riders. There was a brace of current and future Hall of Famers from whom to learn, jockeys like Angel Cordero, Jorge Velasquez, Jose Santos, and Jerry Bailey.

"They made you work for everything," Smith noted. "Just because you were on the best horse didn't mean they were just going to let you gallop around there. If you were going to beat them, you were going to have to earn it. But that polishes you.

"I took to New York really well, and I love it to this day."

Smith opened eyes with his skill, and his outgoing personality won over trainers from whom he needed to get mounts. McGaughey and he reunited and continued doing business together. In 1991, Smith was aboard McGaughey's champion older female Queena. And in 1992 he broke through with his first Breeders' Cup victory when he hustled the McGaughey-trained Lure to the front and made that horse the first wire-to-wire winner in the eight-year history of the Mile.

At the age of 28 in 1993, Smith rose to the top of his profession. After finishing second in the Kentucky Derby with Prairie Bayou, Smith had to zig-zag through the Preakness stretch before gaining a half-length victory with that colt, his first in a Triple Crown race. He also repeated aboard Lure in the Breeders' Cup

Mile, and by year's end had registered a U.S.-record 62 stakes victories, his mounts earning purses of $14,024,815. He won four grade 1 races with Sky Beauty for Hall of Fame trainer Allen Jerkens. Smith received the Eclipse Award as the nation's top jockey for his 1993 season.

"It was amazing," he said. "I was riding really powerful horses—great horses—and I was at the top of my game. When you're riding the quality I was riding, it makes the game awful easy. I was always having fun wherever I was, be it at Sunland Park or in New York. But the thrill of winning the big ones, nothing else is quite like it."

Smith's record of 62 stakes victories in a season lasted exactly one year. In 1994, he improved that tally to 68, with purse earnings of nearly $16 million. Sky Beauty became champion older female that year, and Smith also partnered with a gray time bomb by the name of Holy Bull, with whom he would win eight of 10 starts in 1994 and ride to Horse of the Year honors.

"What a horse," said Smith. "Just a dream. The thing with him was to do as little as possible and stay out of his way. Any movement you gave him—you could wiggle your toe—and he'd respond to it. That's how good he was."

Smith won another pair of Breeders' Cup races in 1995, with Unbridled's Song in the Juvenile and Inside Information in the Distaff, and if it could get any better for Smith, he met Queen Elizabeth II in the winner's circle after Awesome Again won the Queen's Plate at Woodbine in Toronto.

"The Queen said to me, 'Beautiful horse. I think a lot of him.' She loved Awesome Again; she really did. And look at what he turned out to be. [Awesome Again won the 1998 Breeders' Cup Classic and has gone on to become a top sire.] The Queen has an eye for a horse, I'll tell you that," Smith said.

Smith won the Breeders' Cup Classic in 1997 aboard Skip Away, another fearsome gray runner, and the decade seemed to belong to him. Very little goes in a straight line, however, particularly with horses. In March of 1998, Smith was involved in a spill at Gulfstream Park and originally thought he had a broken collarbone, probably the most common of jockey injuries. It turned out, though, he had broken his shoulder in three places.

By August, he had recovered and was on top of the standings at the prestigious summer meet at Saratoga in upstate New York, where he won the Travers Stakes, the most important race for 3-year-olds after the Triple Crown contests, aboard Coronado's Quest. Two days later, in the ninth race on August 31, there was a chain-reaction accident wherein Smith and his mount, Dacron, were forced into the hedge that served as the inside boundary on the turf course. Smith wound up suspended in the bush with two fractured vertebrae.

Smith found himself in a body cast, the silver lining being it could have been even worse. He came back early in 1999 because he wanted to ride in the Kentucky Derby, and had a live mount in the Lukas-trained Cat Thief, finishing third.

"I came back too soon," he said with the benefit of hindsight. "After the Derby, I should have taken off for another month and let myself heal more. I was hurting pretty good, and maybe that showed at times."

There is no guarantee that when a jockey comes back from an extended break he will get the same mounts he had previously. The fact is, other riders will have inherited those horses in the meantime, and one needs to prove himself all over again.

"I was banking on getting the same kind of horses," Smith said. "If I had, maybe I could have gotten back on a roll again and people would have forgotten I'd even been hurt. But I didn't get the horses and I didn't get on the roll. And that's when people really start talking."

It's a chicken-and-egg argument, whether a rider isn't performing as well because of an injury, or whether he isn't performing as well because he's not getting the same quality of horse to ride. Whichever is true, the result is the same: a slump. Smith went to the sidelines again in the latter part of 1999 still trying to heal his back. He reached a low point mentally when three horses he had previously ridden—Cat Thief, Soaring Softly, and Artax—all won Breeders' Cup races that year while he was forced to watch on TV.

"I was spoiled and I didn't even know it," said Smith. "For the first time in my career, riding became work, and I had to fight through it. It's about confidence. When you have more confidence than the other guy, you make the right decisions. There are a million things going on during a race, and they add up. When you get on a roll, you make all the right decisions and always find the right hole to go through."

Smith, though, couldn't get back in the zone in New York. Needing to change something in his routine, he decided to pack his bags for California. Although a known commodity there, Smith was still risking certain headwinds: California doesn't have the benefit of drawing a lot of horses from other jurisdictions and is more of a self-contained island where horse population has traditionally been a problem. And at that time, in 2001, there was a talent-laden jockey colony to contend with, riders like Laffit Pincay Jr., Chris McCarron, Eddie Delahoussaye, Gary Stevens, and Patrick Valenzuela.

"Sometimes change is good," Smith said. "I was just trying to spark something, hoping people would give me a shot. I've been doing this all my life, and I'm a firm believer that when it's your time, it's your time."

After a slow start, Smith's time began to arrive in the latter part of 2001. He began riding for some of the top California outfits, and had an auspicious bridging of the old and new years when he rode Paga to victory in the December 31 Monrovia Handicap for trainer Richard Mandella and then was back in the winner's circle with Snow Ridge in the El Canejo Handicap for Lukas on January 1, 2002. It was a good omen.

Smith picked up the mount on a speedy filly named Azeri in 2002. The daughter of Jade Hunter, bred by Gulfstream Jet founder Allen Paulson and raced by his family after Paulson's death, became a dominant force for the next three seasons, winning 11 grade 1 races and more than $4 million in her 24 lifetime starts, which included 17 victories. In the 2002 Breeders' Cup Distaff, Smith steered Azeri to the front at Arlington International Race Course outside Chicago, cutting through chilling winds to capture the race and earn her the first of three consecutive champion older mare honors. Azeri was also voted Horse of the Year for 2002.

At that same Breeders' Cup at Arlington, Smith had the mount on Vindication, an undefeated colt from one of the last crops of the great Triple Crown winner and top sire Seattle Slew. In his fourth lifetime start, Vindication shot to the fore in the Breeders' Cup Juvenile and dominated 12 other runners, winning by 2¾ lengths under Smith. The trainer of Vindication was none other than Bob Baffert. Although Vindication sustained an injury and would never race again, a bond was forged between trainer and rider.

"That was the first horse I rode for Bob," Smith noted, "and he was undefeated in four races. That's what got me into Bob's barn. With Vindication and Azeri, I got rolling, and good things started happening."

One of those good things was Smith's 2003 induction into racing's Hall of Fame, celebrating his great successes of the 1990s, but also a harbinger of what was still to come.

Another good thing was Smith getting into the barn of trainer John Shirreffs, who began riding Smith steadily. Among Shirreffs' main owners was Jerry Moss, a music-industry executive and the "M" of A&M Records, which he co-founded with trumpeter Herb Alpert. Moss bred his mare Set Them Free to Smith's old mount Holy Bull, getting a gray colt he named Giacomo. Having signed The Police to his label, Moss had named Set Them Free after a song by the band and named Giacomo after a son of lead singer Sting.

Giacomo had shown some talent as a 2-year-old, breaking his maiden early and then finishing second in the grade 1 Hollywood Futurity. As a 3-year-old, he again flashed some ability, but not an overwhelming amount, finishing second in the San Felipe Stakes, a grade 2 event; and fourth in the grade 1 Santa Anita Derby. When he was sent to Kentucky to compete in the Derby, Giacomo still had just a maiden victory to his credit, but Smith had a good feeling about the colt because there was something in him that reminded the rider of Holy Bull. Bettors were far more circumspect, and Giacomo walked into the Kentucky Derby starting gate as a 50-1 shot.

Having finished second in the race three times in his 11 tries prior to 2005, Smith was confident his 12th attempt would be the charm. The first time past the grandstand, that would have been a vast minority opinion. Giacomo left the starting gate with little urgency and settled in next-to-last position while racing five paths off the rail. With a half-mile to go, Smith and Giacomo still had just one horse beat and were 15 lengths behind the leader. At that point, they began picking off some horses while still going wide into the final turn, and with a quarter-mile to go they had advanced into 11th place.

Finding himself behind a wall of horses, Smith steered Giacomo even farther out on the course to gain clear sailing eight paths off the rail. There, Giacomo began a determined rally to the wire, passing Closing Argument late to win by a half-length.

Two years later, the team of Moss, Shirreffs, and Smith would converge again behind a gargantuan Street Cry filly who Moss had named Zenyatta after a Police album. Needing time to grow into her massive frame, Zenyatta didn't make it to the races until late in her 3-year-old season, and Smith rode her to a pair of victories at the end of 2007. As a 4-year-old, Zenyatta won all of her seven races including the Breeders' Cup Distaff (then called the Ladies Classic). At 5, she again took on all comers, winning all five of her races in 2009 and becoming the first, and still only, female to win the Breeders' Cup Classic. She was a perfect 14-for-14 in her career at that point.

What made Zenyatta so exciting for her growing legion of admirers, and so challenging for Smith, was her running style. She showed no early interest in her races, usually dropping back to last place. Smith would have to time her late charge as he guided her to pass horses down the homestretch with a breathless spurt, which increased the thrill level for spectators. Silky Sullivan was another famous come-from-behind runner who amazed fans with his late charge, but Zenyatta carried the extra portfolio of never having been defeated despite her hair-raising running style. Many of her races were decided by less than a length, with Smith always somehow knowing exactly when to time her move.

As a 6-year-old in 2010, Zenyatta won her first five races and traveled to Churchill Downs to defend her crown in the Breeders' Cup Classic. Again, she fell impossibly far behind the remainder of her field, and then on the last turn Smith once more sent her on her way as she flew past her competition. Nearing the wire, she was narrowing the gap between herself and the very good colt Blame, and fans were contorting themselves trying to make their body English get the mare to the line first. This time, though, she fell a head short in the final race of her career. Smith was inconsolable following that finish, blaming himself for not getting the giant mare into action early enough. But the final tally showed what a great run the pair had compiled together: 19 victories in 20 races, $7.3 million in purse earnings, 2010 Horse of the Year crown, three champion older mare titles, and a first-ballot induction to the Hall of Fame.

After Zenyatta, Smith said, "The rest was history. Things really took off."

Smith was then the dean of riders in Southern California, as the rest of his generation retired from the arduous task of steering racehorses. The whispers about him having lost his touch and his bravery had long ago gone silent, and he was sought out to pilot top stock by a variety of trainers. From the Hall of Famer Jerry Hollendorfer, Smith accepted the mount on the brilliant champions Songbird and Shared Belief. But it was Baffert who grew to appreciate Smith's skills more than anyone, and when you're the top gun in Baffert's barn, you are riding more great horses than you would anywhere else west of the Mississippi.

Smith has, since 2015, won stakes on Baffert trainees Game On Dude, Hoppertunity, Mor Spirit, American Anthem, Abel Tasman, Val Dori, West Coast, Drefong, McKinzie, Ax Man, and Marley's Freedom. Mastery may well have threatened the Triple Crown in 2016 had he not gotten hurt after winning a stakes under Smith. When Baffert needed a top rider to guide Arrogate, a late-blooming 3-year-old of 2016, he chose Smith, who partnered with Arrogate to make him the top-earning horse in North American Thoroughbred history.

Smith lets out a chuckle of agreement when he's presented with the theory that very little in life is accomplished in a direct progression. Early success is no guarantee of what is to come around the corner, and so many of Smith's peers have fallen through the trap doors of substance abuse or out-of-control personal lives. Smith has been able to use his own tough spells as a building block, an inspiration, and as valuable experience as he moved forward and put in the hard work necessary to climb back to the top of his profession.

"I truly believe that down time, in some ways, was necessary for me to get to where I am today," he noted. "When I was in my early 20s, I remember Jerry Bailey telling me I was doing good, but that I wasn't going to get really good until I was in my late 30s and 40s. I didn't understand then, but now I know what he meant. There's so much more to it than just being young and feeling good and being able to get down and be strong on a horse. There's a whole other side to it that you learn as you go through the years. Time has to teach you that. You can have people mentoring you and helping you and showing you early so that you catch on quicker than others, but it takes time to really understand it and appreciate it."

When Justify came along, it was a no-brainer for Baffert to go with Smith again, and the jockey knew, as soon as he climbed aboard for that allowance win in Justify's second race, that this could be his ticket to the one thing he had yet to accomplish—winning the coveted Triple Crown.

"I thought he was that kind of horse right away," Smith said. "He dominated that race, and when they do that going around two turns is when you really start getting excited, especially coming up to the Triple Crown races. He could have won by 15 lengths that day if I'd asked him to. And after he handled Bolt d'Oro in the Santa Anita Derby, I thought there was no telling what he could do.

"His mechanics are just amazing. His natural cruising speed is phenomenal, man, and then he's got gears on top of that. And then he had the mind even though he was lightly raced. You only had to show him things once and he got it. He didn't make mistakes. So now you have that talent, and he ain't making no mistakes. You've got a horse this big, this strong, this powerful, and he ain't messing up. He's breaking sharp, putting himself in the race; he's relaxing when you need him to, and responding when you ask him.

"It's not often you get a horse with all that. You get horses with some of that, but not all of that. We need to turn off? I put my hands down. We need to pick up? Pick my hands up and he'd do just what I asked him to do. He actually made my job really easy. It was just fun. You'd think going for the Triple Crown in the Belmont would be a nerve-wracking race for me. But I'll be honest with you: it was probably the least nerve-wracking of the three."

15
RUN-UP TO THE CROWN

WITH THREE WEEKS BETWEEN THE PREAKNESS AND THE
Belmont Stakes, Justify settled in once again at Churchill Downs
to recover from yet another mud bath of a race and prepare for
the third jewel of the Triple Crown. He had exited the Preakness
visibly no worse for wear, but was walked for several days before
heading back to the track for light morning jogs and gallops.

Baffert, with a new crop of 2-year-olds to oversee back at
Santa Anita, might have been physically in California, but his
mind was on his big chestnut colt 2,000 miles away. These are
the nervous days, hoping no ailment comes up, no temperature is
spiked. Every time the cell phone rang, Baffert anxiously checked
the incoming number, hoping it was not the dreaded call from his
assistant Barnes that something, small or large, was not normal
with the big horse.

That call never came. Eight days after the Preakness, Baffert
grabbed a jet to Louisville. The following morning was Memorial
Day, May 28, and Baffert arrived early at Barn 33 at Churchill
Downs to assess Justify. Exercise rider Gomez would be charged
that morning with putting the colt to a strong gallop, after which
Baffert would decide whether to give Justify an official workout
the following day.

As always with Justify, time was tight. Unlike between the Kentucky Derby and Preakness, Baffert knew he had to get some serious work into his horse to prepare him for the rigors of the Belmont Stakes, a 1½-mile journey so rigorous for young horses it is known as "The Test of a Champion." Many top horses have failed in the final leg of the Triple Crown, the third tough race for these 3-year-olds in just a five-week span. Horse after horse have won the Derby and Preakness, and then, with visions of a Triple Crown dancing in everyone's head, failed to seal the deal in New York. Baffert has lost the Belmont three times with horses going for the Triple Crown, and he wanted to make sure Justify went into that gunfight with weapons blazing. If all went to plan, Baffert desired to give him two timed workouts before the Belmont to keep the horse as sharp as possible.

As Justify was being walked around the barn prior to emerging for the short walk to the Churchill track, Baffert bounced out from the shadows of the barn in good spirits. His preliminary check of Justify had gone well, the horse having held his weight through the first two Triple Crown races, and now trainer and horse were heading for the homestretch.

A couple dozen onlookers, mainly photographers with a smattering of reporters and fans mixed in, followed along behind Justify as he made his way to the track under Gomez, accompanied by Barnes on a pony. Baffert took up his station at the gap at the edge of the racetrack and was soon joined by a familiar figure on horseback. Wayne Lukas was out on the track watching a set of his runners train, including Bravazo, the Preakness runner-up who would join Justify as the only two horses this year to run in all three Triple Crown races. Lukas backed his pony up to the outside rail, and he and Baffert exchanged pleasantries for several minutes before Lukas moved off to attend to his runners.

Justify came galloping past Baffert shortly thereafter. Baffert honed in on the horse, but he can tell only so much visually. Additional valuable intel was going to come from Gomez.

"I flew in because I wanted to see him gallop," Baffert said. "I told Humberto if he felt anything at all different in the horse, to let me know. Humberto is really good, one of the best. He works with the horses and makes them use all their muscles, and he lets me know what's going on. I told him if Justify feels at all lethargic, then don't do too much with him. I wanted to know if he was ready to work the next day, or whether he needed more time."

Gomez had more on his mind than galloping Justify, however. Just before the Preakness his father, who had been sick back in Mexico, died. Even if he had left immediately, there was no guarantee Gomez would have gotten back to his village in time for the funeral, and he had a tough decision to make.

"The reason I'm in the horse industry is because my dad was a big fan of racing," Gomez said. "He was sick but he managed to watch the Kentucky Derby, and I know he was proud, because that was a dream come true for us.

"It was a sad moment when he passed. By the time I would have gotten there, it would have all been done. So I decided to stay because it was important to me to see this through, and it was important to him as well. So I think it was the right decision to stay with the horse, and it is something I will never forget. I have worked with horses my whole life, and it was hard work to get to this point, and I am very thankful and humble about it."

Having pulled Justify up, Gomez brought the colt back to the gap where Baffert awaited them. Before Baffert could raise the question, Gomez looked down at the trainer from his perch on Justify's back and stated, "This horse wants to work."

Perhaps seeking inspiration for the upcoming Belmont, Baffert agreed to travel to Lexington and visit American Pharoah again that day for a feature segment NBC wanted to shoot for its Belmont Stakes show. Accompanied by *Sports Illustrated*'s fine writer Tim Layden, whose beat for the magazine includes horse racing, Baffert made the hour-long drive to Ashford Stud. Walking a short way from the parking area down toward Ashford's stallion complex, Baffert was greeted by American Pharoah outside the barn.

Said Layden, "Baffert stroked his mane and patted him on the face, and said, 'This is what we miss with Justify. With him, it's five seconds and then he wants you out of his face.' Bob must have stood there for 20 minutes, rubbing Pharoah's back and hindquarters, and reminisced about his racing career and the differences between the two horses."

American Pharoah is a unique horse in that he never turns away human interaction. It's as though he's got some Labrador retriever mixed in with his Thoroughbred blood. He, not Justify, is the outlier in this respect. Justify is not a mean horse but will tolerate only so much handling.

Baffert kept on with his monologue for the cameras. "He did some unbelievable things," he continued about Pharoah. "What sticks with me is the shipping: to Oaklawn, back to California, to Kentucky, Baltimore, Kentucky, New York, California, New Jersey, California, New York, Kentucky. And he brought it every single time. Let's see if Justify can do that."

Said Layden, "He was clearly emotional, and his voice cracked a couple of times. When they walked American Pharoah back to the barn, Lookin At Lucky [a Baffert Preakness winner] was in there, in a stall caddy-corner to Pharoah's. Bob patted Pharoah on the nose again on his way out. He was moved being around the horse, no doubt about that. You could see the personal relationship there."

Gomez was certainly right about Justify wanting to work. The following day, on Tuesday, May 29, 10 days after the Preakness and 11 days before the Belmont Stakes, Justify breezed a half-mile at Churchill Downs clocked in a rapid :46 and four-fifths. Normally, that fast a work would give a trainer a case of indigestion that an entire bottle of Tums wouldn't make a dent in, but Justify clearly was not a normal horse. Bottled up since the Preakness, he was ready to expend energy, and this was just another sign of how good a horse he was, and how well he was doing. There were no worries about him wasting such a strong effort during training rather than in his next race, and so Baffert was able to wing back to California knowing the horse had come out of the Preakness perfectly, and cleared one more hurdle toward the ultimate goal.

Six days later, on June 4, the Monday before the Belmont, Baffert was back at Churchill Downs to supervise Justify's final workout before the race. He wanted more distance and less speed this time, and brought along jockey Martin Garcia to work Justify. The official clockers timed Justify for five furlongs, giving him a 1:01 and two-fifths workout, but Baffert had ordered Garcia to keep going longer on the colt, who covered six furlongs in 1:13 and three-fifths and seven furlongs in 1:27 and one-fifth before being pulled up.

Having sensed how keen the colt was in his previous workout, Baffert, going by feel, allowed him to really clear out his lungs with this work.

"He's basically run himself into shape here," the trainer noted. "Martin said he didn't even take a deep breath. All seems good."

Justify walked the barn the following day, then on Wednesday, June 6, he strode onto a van for the short ride to the Louisville airport and then a flight to MacArthur Airport in Islip, Long Island, about an hour's drive from Belmont Park.

Rick Samuels, a freelance photographer who has shot major races for *BloodHorse* magazine for two decades, also takes marketing photos for the Brook Ledge Horse Transportation company, a unique position that allows him access to certain legs of journeys closed to other media members. Samuels, who has also trained racehorses and rodeo horses, was waiting for Justify at MacArthur, and took the horse-van ride with the colt from the airport to Belmont Park that afternoon.

"He stepped off the plane and walked into the van like he'd done it a million times," Samuels said. "There was some commotion, but it was all caused by people from the airport wanting to jump in the van and get a picture with him. One woman came on carrying flowers; she was trying to give the flowers to Justify and hitting him in the nose with them, and he's trying to eat them. There was some merriment when she fell off the ramp getting off the van.

"But the horse was like, 'Whatever.' Hoppertunity [a 7-year-old graded stakes winner trained by Baffert] was in the back of the van with [groom] Eduardo Luna holding him, and Jimmy [Barnes] was in front holding Justify. I've been on vans with horses where, if you hit a bump, they lose their minds. Or one horse starts acting up, so they all start acting up. This horse was completely relaxed. You would have never known he was a young horse who had only been running a few months.

"It was about an hour ride and Justify looked out the window. Before I got on the van, I thought he was going to win the race. After seeing him, I *knew* he was going to win, just by his mentality. He was like one of my rope horses going on a van to a rodeo. They'll stand on the van 15 hours, get off, and go rope a few calves. He seemed that laid-back, cool, and calm. 'Just load me in the gate and let's run the race.'"

About 100 members of the media were staked outside Barn 1 on the Belmont Park backstretch by mid-afternoon, the savvier photographers perched on small stepladders to get a clear vantage point. Justify was fashionably late, by at least an hour from the scheduled time of his arrival. Since he's been coming to the Belmont, Baffert has stabled his horses in the barn of John and Tonya Terranova, who had moved from Barn 7, near the gap to the racetrack, to Barn 1, closest to Hempstead Turnpike on the northern edge of the Belmont property. Baffert and Elliott Walden stood nervously together outside the barn, checking their cell phones, Baffert no doubt in touch with his assistant Barnes on the van.

Shortly before 3:00 PM the Brook Ledge van pulled up outside the barn, and Samuels jumped out to gain a good spot from which to shoot Justify getting off the vehicle. After the ramp was put in place and rails assembled at its sides, Justify was led off the van by Barnes, who immediately handed him over to Baffert. As the photographers clicked away, Baffert brought the horse inside the barn, which has two long aisles so that horses can be walked around inside it in a large oval pattern. Baffert wanted to take a few laps with Justify, giving himself a chance to eyeball the colt and see how he was moving. After several go-arounds, Baffert handed the colt off, and assistants continued to exercise him until he was inserted in his stall.

Baffert then came back outside the barn to address the media. Unlike athletes in other sports who now are taught how to handle interviews and what to say and not say, racehorse trainers have nothing to go on but their instincts. They handle the task of publicizing their star runners with varying degrees of success, with some bristling at the invasion of privacy as they try to go about their daily work. Racing is a sport that by and large lacks for good publicity. It is constantly trying to play catch-up and upgrade the public's relatively poor perception of it. Yet as much as the sport needs to improve its image, many of its participants have no idea how to handle the spotlight when it shines on them.

Baffert is the exception. He has flown to the light like a moth to flame from the beginning, and well knows the chore that he faces as he moves to a microphone set up by New York Racing Association officials to address the media horde outside Barn 1. He speaks all in generalities; the horse is settling in and looking good, which is evident from his appearance. He re-states some version of those perceptions through 20 minutes of questioning.

Justify is still the picture of a gorgeous Thoroughbred after his travels and that day's trip from Louisville to New York. Baffert has two days to get the colt acclimated to this racetrack, which by its composition has more of a sand content than most others, hence its nickname of "Big Sandy." At a mile and a half around, it is also the largest racetrack in North America, and the Belmont Stakes will entail exactly one historic circuit of the layout.

After dispatching his duty of giving the press something to file following Justify's arrival, Baffert repairs back inside the barn to check on his horse again. Outside, the photographers break down their equipment and head back across a parking lot to the Belmont Park grandstand, where they will upload their photos in a ground-floor room next to the tunnel that connects the saddling paddock to the racetrack.

Barn 1 returns to normal, and just a couple of reporters remain some 15 minutes after the end of the press conference. Baffert, his shirtsleeves rolled up, emerges from the barn and walks over to a short wooden fence with a couple of horizontal rails. He is out of "official" mode now, and just having a conversation. *SI*'s Layden, Dave Grening from *Daily Racing Form,* and I are the only reporters around. Baffert is amazed at what he's just seen, and it's something he didn't share while at the microphone.

While he was walking Justify around the shedrow, the horses already ensconced in the barn came to the front of their stalls and began hollering at the new arrival.

"It was like he was giving off a vibe," Baffert said of Justify, "and the other horses started screaming. I've never had a horse before where horses in the barn went nuts like that."

The conversation turned toward the ascension of Justify at the same time that McKinzie had been forced to the sidelines, and then a reminiscence about Baffert's late friend Brad McKinzie, who was at his side from his early days training Quarter Horses on forward to his death two years ago.

"People who knew him are always asking me what Brad would have thought about the way this has turned out," said Baffert, "with McKinzie getting hurt and Justify emerging. He would have said, 'McKinzie wouldn't want any part of that big red s.o.b. anyway.'"

These days in New York leading up to the Belmont would be far different than Baffert's previous tries at winning the Triple Crown. Even though American Pharoah turned the trick in 2015, nobody would have been taking that for granted in the week before that race. And after three failed attempts by Baffert trainees, the pressure was even greater with American Pharoah, because the Triple Crown drought had reached 37 years and fans of the sport were wondering whether a Triple Crown was now an impossible dream beyond the abilities of the modern Thoroughbred. So many followers of horse racing had never seen one in their lifetimes, and its difficulty had reached legendary status.

Ultimately, though, American Pharoah broke through, and that set this journey with Justify apart from previous ones for his connections.

"It was night and day, this time versus Pharoah," said Jill Baffert. "There was so much pressure with Pharoah. It was the fourth time Bob was going for the Triple Crown, and there was a feeling that if you don't grab it and capture it, you're never going to get another opportunity. With Justify, we were still kind of in disbelief. It all happened so fast with him. But it was definitely more relaxed, like it's gravy from here on in."

That didn't mean the superstitions had gone away, however. The Bafferts were in a grocery store a couple of days before the race and paid for their purchase with a $100 bill. The clerk gave them a $50 bill back as part of their change. Fifty-dollar bills, at least at one time, were considered bad luck around the racetrack.

"We had to tell her we couldn't take that bill; that we needed smaller change," Jill said. "You could see she was telling her co-workers the story, and that they were looking at us like we were crazy. We tried to tell them we were from the racetrack, and that there's no way we could accept a $50 bill right then."

The trainer acknowledged that the $50-bill superstition was an old one he'd heard about around the racetrack, but at this particular moment, he was just being sure about covering all bases.

"I've won some races and afterward looked in my wallet and saw $50 bills," he said. "So that isn't a big deal anymore. The main one for me is a black cat. We were in Manhattan the day before the Belmont and we went to a candy store. I look in the window and see these black cat chocolates, and I was like, 'Get... those...things...away...from...me.' That's the only black cat I saw that week. I got out of there in a hurry. But if I would have gotten beat, I would have blamed them."

Baffert did all the public relations events on the New York circuit leading up to the race. He rang the opening bell at the New York Stock Exchange one morning and threw out the first pitch at a New York Mets game.

"I was really enjoying it more this time," noted Baffert. "It had already been done. If Pharoah hadn't won it, I probably would have been like, 'Oh, man, we have to go through this again.' But I loved Justify's last work at Churchill Downs. He was so strong, and I was happy with that, and he came out of that really well. When we got to Belmont and we took him to the track for the first time Thursday morning, I could tell he got over the surface well and came back well, and I felt confident we just needed racing luck and he could get it done.

"We made a conscious effort to hit some more parties than usual and just relax, not having to be so uptight all the time. Everything went so smoothly, and everybody was having a good time. Jill got to meet [*The Tonight Show* host] Jimmy Fallon, who she loves. And I really felt good about the horse, because every day he looked better and better there. The day before the race, when Justify came off the track, he was like a tiger. I was playing it down in interviews, but we were extremely confident."

After going with Justify to the track for his gallops in the two mornings leading up to the race, and then watching him cool out back at the barn, Baffert dutifully marched over to the grandstand and gave a daily mid-morning press conference, set up so that media members could all be taken care of in one session. Again, Baffert handled it all professionally, although he was asked the same questions each day and gave the same answers. The horse looked good. He seemed to like the racetrack. And he had similarities to and differences from American Pharoah. There wasn't much more to say, and certainly little that could be asked or answered that hadn't been gone over before.

One question did intrigue Baffert a bit, though. Justify, who had carried the WinStar silks in his previous two Triple Crown races, would run under the China Horse Club silks in the Belmont. Baffert denied being superstitious about that change, but seemed amused by it, turning to *BloodHorse*'s Steve Haskin to ask if that had ever happened before with a Triple Crown winner (it hadn't).

Leaning up against a wall in the makeshift press conference room the day before the race was trainer Dale Romans, who would be saddling Free Drop Billy in the Belmont. When a reporter sidled up and asked Romans if he was on a spying mission, the trainer snorted. "I'm waiting for [wife] Tammy [Fox] to get out of the bathroom," he said.

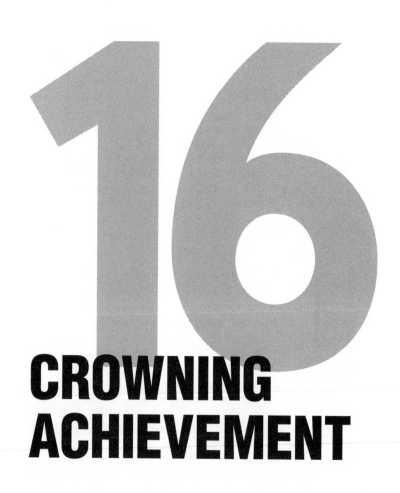

16
CROWNING
ACHIEVEMENT

GOOD MAGIC, NOT ESPECIALLY SUITED TO THE BELMONT'S extra distance and needing a break after the first two legs of the Triple Crown, was sitting out the race. But nine other horses were signed up to take a crack at Justify in the Belmont Stakes, their connections emboldened by the visual image of the colt's diminishing advantage in the final strides of the Preakness. Even had they been privy to Smith's encouraging explanation to Baffert for the closeness of that finish, they likely would have chosen not to believe it.

Lukas, never one to back down from a challenge, sent Bravazo back out to do battle in the Belmont. Tenfold, who was also closing late in the Preakness to finish third, just a neck behind Bravazo, was back as well. Gronkowski, a muscular colt built like his namesake, the pro football tight end Rob Gronkowski, had earned a berth in the Derby through his European exploits but couldn't make that race because of injury. He showed up at the Belmont though, having been switched to the barn of Chad Brown. Brown was encouraged by the little he'd seen of Gronkowski but given his short training time with the colt—about a week—didn't truly know what to expect from him.

Noble Indy, co-owned by WinStar and one of Justify's training mates during his early days at that farm, reappeared in the

Belmont after having run 17th in the Derby. Vino Rosso, also no stranger to Justify, going even further back with him to the fields of Glennwood Farm where they were both raised, was here. Hofburg, from the international powerhouse Juddmonte Farms, had encountered traffic problems in the Derby but ran on well, and it was thought the Belmont's longer distance would only help him. Baffert had a second horse in the field in Restoring Hope, although that was a decision more attributable to his owners, Gary and Mary West, longtime clients of the trainer's. And Romans' Free Drop Billy rounded out the field.

Thankfully, June 9 dawned with no rain in the forecast, no excessive heat, nothing potentially game-changing from Mother Nature. Fans streamed into Belmont Park all day, total attendance limited to around 90,000 by New York Racing Association officials. Belmont is slated for renovation soon after the running of the 2018 Belmont, and there is ample need for it. The facilities are outdated and had not stood up to recent crowds. Fourteen years before, when Smarty Jones tried for the Triple Crown, 120,000 fans descended on Belmont, busting the track. Pipes ruptured, toilets stopped working, and there was little running water at the plant. NYRA executives subsequently decided to cap future Belmont days at the 90,000 figure. That attendance is only approached in the years when a Triple Crown is on the line. In recent non–Triple Crown years, about 60,000-65,000 fans make it for the Belmont Stakes.

At a Manhattan hotel, the Baffert family, including several of Bob's children from his first marriage, prepared to depart for the track in late morning.

"We were going to leave the hotel at 11:00," remembered Jill, "and we just kept putting it off and putting it off. It's almost like we didn't want to know the outcome."

In 2017, Baffert did not have a horse in the Belmont Stakes, but he still managed to assault New York as if he were King Kong, winning four stakes races on the Belmont Stakes undercard. On Belmont Day 2018, Baffert again didn't have to worry about "stinking up the place." He won the Ogden Phipps Stakes with Abel Tasman and the Brooklyn Invitational Stakes with Justify's van mate Hoppertunity, so there were no worries about the barn going cold at the worst possible time.

Walden was nervous and confident at the same time leading up to the race. In contrast to Super Saver, who had lost his appetite going through the Triple Crown series, and Victory Gallop, who Walden had trained to a Belmont win in spite of a skin disease and lost weight, Justify was giving no signs of tailing off.

"There's usually something going on," Walden said. "It's so rare that a horse can never have a bad day but Justify was that way. Other than a bump or a bruise, whenever he hit the racetrack, he gave you confidence."

Thirty minutes before the Belmont Stakes, up in the first row of box seats opposite the 16th pole, breeder John Gunther sat relaxed, talking into his cell phone. Gunther's work had long since been completed, but this day, this moment, was all his doing. Thirteen years before he had seen something he liked in the Pulpit mare Magical Illusion in the sale pavilion, and he and his daughter subsequently set in motion the matings that led to Magical Illusion's grandson, who was the star of this show.

Gunther ended his call and came to stand against the rail of the box seat area with a reporter who'd done a long piece on him months before. Unlike at Churchill Downs, he was enjoying the hospitality at Belmont, and had for company his daughter, Tanya, and his good friend Steve Irwin. Tanya had gone back to the paddock to see their onetime babies Justify and Vino Rosso.

John Gunther was smiling and confident, a proud parent about to watch what he hoped was the coronation of his child.

"We've been at the track most of the day," he said. "We got to see Vino Rosso earlier, but we didn't see Justify today because of all the security around the barn. It's a special, unbelievable day. I'm not nervous; I don't know why. I'm super-confident. He was so special off the farm, and he continues to look better and better all the time."

Baffert, after saddling Justify, took up residence in the boxes as well. This was the only one of the three Triple Crown races this year he would watch live out on the racetrack. He never did say in public what he felt deep within, that he thought his horse was so good that the result was a foregone conclusion. If there was any uncertainty in his mind, it was because of tactics potentially being employed by some of his competitors to try and compromise Justify's chances.

"You could hear and sense some hostility. There was chirping going on," Baffert would say months after the race. "People were talking about rabbits and how they weren't going to let him get away. With Pharoah, there wasn't any of that, but with this horse I could sense a lot of it."

Employing a rabbit is racetrack terminology for someone to send a very fast horse out to the front early in a race, either to set a fast pace to make it easier for a come-from-behind runner, or to compromise a fast horse like Justify by running alongside him early trying to prompt him to increase his speed and therefore drain his tank, also setting the stage for a late-running horse to go by him down the stretch.

This particular Belmont field presented an intricate spider-web of intrigue and intertwined interests whose cross purposes would lead to various ramifications long after the running of the race. Here was the manifestation of what can happen with the advent of partnerships dominating the ownership of racehorses. You couldn't tell the players' interests without a program, and a rather large diagram.

The first matter of intrigue involved a horse not even in the race. Audible, who had closed resolutely to be third in the Kentucky Derby, had not been entered in either the Preakness or the Belmont Stakes. He was the horse who Jack Wolf and Sol Kumin had both bought into along with Justify from WinStar, SF, and China Horse Club. But Wolf and Kumin, like their deal in Justify, only had an interest in Audible's racing career, not his breeding career, so the only way they could recoup their investment in him is if he ran in races and earned purse money. Audible was said to have sustained an injury in or after the Derby, but the nature of that injury had not been made public and was a mystery even to his minority owners.

Wolf and Kumin would have preferred to see Audible going for part of the $1.5 million Belmont purse, and had to be wondering whether Justify's presence in the race influenced the majority owners not to run Audible. Months later Kumin said he'd been informed—after the Belmont—that Audible had come out of the Kentucky Derby with some minor bone-bruising, and the colt had been sent back to WinStar Farm. Audible did not return to the races until November 3, when he won a minor stakes event at Churchill Downs, so surely there was something amiss with him.

Left to his own devices, Baffert would not have started Restoring Hope in the Belmont, but owners Gary and Mary West felt the horse was bred to get the distance, and he had been training well. In his previous race, the Pat Day Mile at Churchill Downs on Derby Day, Restoring Hope had been taken off the pace and did not enjoy getting dirt kicked back into his face. The plan in the Belmont, then, was to have him sit up near the front close to, but behind, Justify, because he possessed some natural speed.

Then came the case of WinStar Farm and New York–based owner Mike Repole. WinStar, which bred Noble Indy, had brought Repole in as a co-owner of the horse. Repole was also the co-owner of Vino Rosso, the Gunther-bred colt whose running style was that of a confirmed closer. Noble Indy, winner of the Louisiana Derby in front-running fashion, had run poorly in the Kentucky Derby, packing it in after seven furlongs and finishing a well-beaten 17th.

WinStar, shooting for the Triple Crown with Justify, would not have been gung-ho to run Noble Indy in the Belmont at all, certainly not after his Derby performance. Vino Rosso hadn't set the Derby on fire either, but he did pass some horses late to finish ninth and was likely the better prospect between Repole's two Belmont horses. Elliott Walden and Repole engaged in a lengthy discussion leading up to the Belmont about whether Noble Indy should be entered in the race and, if he was, how he should be ridden. Walden's concern was that he not be entered simply as a rabbit, an early speed threat to Justify, therefore potentially compromising Justify while also setting up the race for Repole's other entry, the late-running Vino Rosso.

"I would not have run Noble Indy if we owned him outright," stated Walden months later. "But we try to accommodate our partners in these horses, and so if Mike wanted to run, I wanted to acquiesce and run him—under the conditions that he be ridden to try and win the race and not be used as a rabbit.

"The thing was, Mike's belief was the only way for Noble Indy to win the race was for him to be on the lead because he'd won the Louisiana Derby that way, so in his mind he felt it wasn't a rabbit-type situation as much as it was the best thing for the horse. I explained my position, which was if the race goes [a

quarter-mile] in :22 and [a half-mile] :45, it's not in his best interest to be on the lead trying to go a mile and a half. That to me
made no sense, and that's where we disagreed."

Walden, whether he knew it or not, was receiving backup
from jockey Florent Geroux, who had ridden Noble Indy in the
Kentucky Derby and was aboard Restoring Hope in the Belmont.
Geroux felt that Noble Indy wasn't fast enough early to be able to
run with Justify, or even with Restoring Hope.

No matter the plans of others, Baffert knew exactly where he
wanted Justify in the early stages of the race: on the lead.

"When we drew the 1 hole, we knew Mike had to leave," said
Baffert. "I didn't want a Big Brown situation [Big Brown won the
first two legs of the 2008 Triple Crown series before famously fal-
tering in the Belmont] where he drew the rail in the Belmont and
hesitated leaving the gate, and the next thing you know they've
got you pinned in and they're bouncing you around. Boxing us in
was going to be the only shot the others had. They were all going
to try and corral us leaving there."

High above the track as the horses moved into the starting
gate, track announcer Larry Collmus prepared his audience,
reminding it of the stakes at hand. "Justify is in stall 1," he
intoned. "Will he take his place in history?"

And then the gates sprung open.

"Mike left there like he was going 440 yards with a Quarter
Horse," said Baffert of the start. "He was down on his belly and
sent him hard."

Smith wasn't the only one riding hard for early position,
however. From post 9, Javier Castellano pumped on Noble Indy
trying to drive him up toward the front. Luis Saez on Bravazo also
asked his mount for speed from post 3. And Geroux demanded
early run from Restoring Hope, pointing him between horses
and up toward the front. Restoring Hope, perhaps surprised by

the early encouragement, got rank and began running erratically, lugging out toward the outside as the field approached the first turn. Castellano wasn't able to get Noble Indy out as quickly as he may have wanted to, and couldn't get on equal terms with Bravazo, much less Justify, who was a length and a half in front of Bravazo into the first turn.

In the days after the race, Repole asked the Belmont Park stewards to investigate the running of the race, specifically whether Restoring Hope had interfered purposely with Noble Indy. While clear of Noble Indy, Restoring Hope had cut in front of him as he lugged out. The stewards declined to take up Repole's request. Todd Pletcher, the trainer of Noble Indy, would not use the early portion of the race as an excuse.

"Noble Indy didn't behave great in the paddock," he said. "He got a bit anxious in the post parade, and then he didn't break great. He broke out a little bit, and Javier decided to do something different than what we set out to do, and the horse didn't respond very well."

Geroux got Restoring Hope settled down and sat outside of Justify and a length behind him. He was slightly ahead of Bravazo, who set up camp directly behind Justify. Noble Indy remained in the four-path around the turn and up the backstretch. Justify had settled into his familiar easy rhythm, though he was moving at a good clip, getting the first quarter-mile in :23.37 and the half in :48.11, spry for the lengthy distance of the Belmont. Smith liked everything about his journey to that point.

"I felt so blessed going into the race to have that opportunity, and I wanted to enjoy the experience and have fun trying," he said. "I felt all I had to do was get him out of the gate running and put him into the race and see where we're at. I thought he would be on the lead, and he was. He ran pretty quickly the first quarter because I rode him out of there pretty hard. But again, that's where his intelligence comes in. I put my hands down once he established the lead, and he flicked his ears up, took a deep breath of air, and just slowed down.

"He got into that comfortable rhythm and I thought, 'Oh, man.' I had to keep reminding myself to stay focused and stop smiling."

Unhurried and with nobody coming along to challenge him, Justify was allowed to run easily on his own, and the fractions began to get kinder to him, as he ran the first six furlongs—the halfway point of the Belmont—in 1:13.21.

"I was just watching the clock the whole way around there," said Baffert. "I knew the clock was going to be my friend or my enemy."

After Justify crossed the one-mile mark in 1:38.09 with a two-length lead, the picture started changing. Noble Indy came under a ride, Castellano going to his stick early, but the horse offered no response. He began dropping out through the field. Restoring Hope was empty as well, and Bravazo, although still game, ceded his position on the second turn as John Velazquez made his move with Vino Rosso, who took up the chase. Belmont Park's turns go on forever compared to other racetracks, making it difficult for jockeys from out of town to know exactly when to ask their mounts. Velazquez, though, has been a top rider in New York for years, and he roused Vino Rosso with three-eighths of a mile to run. Vino Rosso got to within a length of Justify on that sweeping turn, but a closer look revealed Velazquez riding him hard, even going to the stick on the turn, while Smith was still sitting quietly on Justify, not asking him yet to shift gears.

"I could tell by the way Mike was riding that he had so much horse," said Baffert. "His usual move is to open up just outside the quarter pole. But I had told him the day before not to do that.

I wanted him to wait and straighten out for home off the turn before he asked him."

Smith remembered that conversation as he approached the quarter pole. "I was saying to myself, 'Don't do anything you don't have to do. Don't ask him for too much. Just go with the flow.' So I just kept hand-riding him."

Gronkowski, who had dropped out to dead last early in the race and still trailed Justify by nine lengths with a half-mile to run, found his best stride coming off the turn. He was flying down at the rail, cut the corner sharply, moved inside Vino Rosso, and got to within two lengths of Justify. Vino Rosso continued on gamely, but he'd already busted his best move and wasn't able to get on terms with the leader.

With a furlong to run, Smith knew he didn't need to conserve any more of Justify's energy, and he applied the first of four right-handed reminders to the colt's flank. The crowd waited breathlessly, nervously wondering if Justify had still more to give.

"I was sitting in the box next to Chad Brown, who had Gronkowski," said Jack Wolf. "And coming down the stretch, I could see Chad getting excited while I started looking for the wire. That can be a bad combination."

Where others had wilted in the last furlong of the 12-furlong Belmont Stakes, however, Justify never wavered, carrying on like a powerful metronome, running with precision as he repeated his stride in powerful rhythm. Gronkowski was game, but he was no longer closing the gap between himself and Justify. On the outside, Hofburg came running late, passing Vino Rosso. But he was never going to threaten the leader.

As 90,327 patrons screamed encouragement, Justify proceeded with inevitable sureness down toward the wire. Track announcer Collmus put down his binoculars as Justify ran inside the eighth pole, and, with his left arm chopping the air repeatedly, he too seemed to be urging the colt to the finish. As Justify completed his journey, Collmus screamed, "He's just perfect, and now he's just immortal…Justify has done it!"

Justify reached history's doorstep in 2:28:18, besting Gronkowski by 1¾ lengths. Hofburg finished the same margin in back of the runner-up and a neck in front of Vino Rosso. Noble Indy checked in last of the 10, defeated by more than 54 lengths. After all of the strategizing and maneuvering, the result of the Belmont confirmed that the best horse had won.

The roar that washed down from the grandstand chased Justify through the stretch and back around the clubhouse turn. Grand old Belmont was as loud as any other stadium has gotten for any sporting event. Even after going a mile and a half, Justify was a handful and wasn't yet ready to be pulled up until he had galloped well onto the backstretch. Smith hung his head down low near the colt's neck as if in prayer, not responding to the outrider who had grabbed hold of Justify and congratulated the jockey.

When Smith brought Justify back around in front of the crowd, he continued on with him past the winner's circle and up toward the end of the grandstand so that as many witnesses as possible could get a close-up look at the 13th Triple Crown winner, and just the second (Seattle Slew) to accomplish it while undefeated.

Baffert, too, joined exclusive company, moving alongside Brooklyn native James "Sunny Jim" Fitzsimmons, who had spent 78 years on the racetrack, as the only trainers to have won two Triple Crowns. Baffert also hurdled over Lukas, 15 to 14, as the trainer with the most victories in Triple Crown races.

As is the norm of the day, applause took a backseat to screaming in the grandstand, as the patrons' hands were busy lifting up their cell phones to take pictures and videos of Justify as he passed them heading back to the winner's circle near the finish line. The mania wasn't as pitched as it had been three years earlier for American Pharoah, but that is the difference between three seasons and 37. Enjoyment replaced disbelief this time. Emotions, however, still ran high. Horse racing doesn't have the raw number of fans as the major U.S. team sports do, but the ones it does have are emotionally invested in it. And when an athlete reaches the sport's pinnacle, it touches something deep inside, and eyes well up and tear as history is written before them. It is at these moments that horse racing's problems and its negative perception among the general public fall away, replaced by ecstasy and a celebration of all that can be noble in the sport, personified by a perfect specimen who represents the finest that centuries of breeding can offer.

There is no better place than New York for an experience like the Triple Crown. The state remains the keystone of the U.S. horse racing world, and its fans are the most knowledgeable and appreciative of the sport's history. Each Belmont Stakes week, connections of the great Secretariat descend on Belmont Park, meeting fans and signing autographs on photos and memorabilia just inside the grandstand. Forty-five years after his Triple Crown, Secretariat's fans still dutifully queue up to greet jockey Ron Turcotte, and in years past, exercise rider Charlie Davis and owner Penny Chenery, both of whom had passed away in the year before Justify's run. When Chenery was present, the line of admirers waiting to have a word and share a memory with her stretched half a football field back through the grandstand alongside the lines at the mutuel windows. New Yorkers don't forget greatness. And they don't forget history.

Collmus expressed the passion hanging in the air right after the race. "It was and wasn't different this time," he said. "With American Pharoah, you can't match the fact it had been

37 years, with so many close calls. The moment he hit the wire was completely overwhelming. There were three cameras in the announcer's booth, and I had to run away from them and hide because I was bawling. I'd been a fan forever and calling races since I was 18, and it hits you that you just called a horse winning the Triple Crown.

"Fast-forward three years and it's not going to be quite that, but it was still pretty overwhelming; pretty fantastic. I didn't have that moment in the booth where I was overcome, but a short time later I walked down to the NBC trailers in the parking lot, and everybody was high-fiving, and I remember walking into a trailer, and [NBC show host] Laffit Pincay III was in there, and I broke down. I needed somebody to understand why I lost it again. It took longer for that moment to happen, but they were both very special."

Kumin had a few dozen family members and friends at the Belmont. "I cried when the horse crossed the finish line, which I never thought would happen," he said. "Just looking at the people around me and the emotion and what we were a part of was great."

Baffert, who had been trapped in a chaotic crowd three years earlier, had a game plan in place this time. When Justify hit the wire, he told the owners of Justify, some of whom were seated around him, not to hesitate, and they headed quickly down toward the winner's circle.

"I just wanted to see this great horse and thank him. He's such a big, noble-looking horse," said Baffert. "I had my escape route planned this time. We were ready. I wanted to get down to the track immediately because I wanted to meet Mike when he got back there. I couldn't wait to see the look on his face. And when he brought the horse back I said, 'Welcome to the club.'"

Smith had been able to keep the idea of winning the Triple Crown out of his head during the race as he stayed focused on the job at hand. But it hit him in the moments afterward.

"These waves of emotion just roll over you, man," he said. "I didn't even know who I was talking to. I just wanted to hug everybody that was around me. It was the greatest, humblest, peaceful feeling in the world. Just unbelievable. I wish everyone would have an opportunity to feel that.

"I told Bob I wanted to hug the horse and asked him if I could get off him, and he said, 'No, just stay up there.' And I thought back to winning my first Breeders' Cup race with Lure, and I couldn't stop pumping my fists afterward. [Claiborne Farm president] Seth Hancock said, 'I know you're happy and we're all excited, but you don't have to do all that. The horse is tired and has run hard.' And that stuck in my head, and after that if I did celebrate, I'd hardly move.

"I've been blessed to have ridden some great horses in my career, and Bob has been a part of a lot of that. We've accomplished a lot of goals, but this time he helped me accomplish a dream."

"Mike was wanting to cry," remembered Baffert. "He was so terrific during the whole thing. He took care of Justify, warmed him up right, pulled him up right, and let him catch his breath before bringing him back to the winner's circle. He's a good horseman and he loves the horses. There are jockeys that are great athletes, but they don't have the horsemanship. He has it. And he knew this horse was his ticket to the Promised Land."

Baffert then proceeded to lose it while being interviewed on NBC. In the years before Pharoah's Triple Crown both of the trainer's parents had died, and before Justify's he had lost his friend McKinzie, and all that emotion caught up with him. "I'm getting help from upstairs," he said. "They're giving me that little push. Things happen for a reason. If it's meant to be, it's meant to be. And this is such a magnificent animal."

Said NYRA's Martin Panza, "When American Pharoah won the Triple Crown it was the greatest day of racing that I've ever witnessed; the roar from that crowd. But even though it had been done three years ago, everybody recognizes how extremely difficult the Triple Crown is to accomplish, and everyone realizes how incredible it is for a horse to break his maiden and then in 111 days win the Triple Crown. That shows a great amount of brilliance on Justify's part, and a great job done by Bob."

The post–Belmont Stakes press conference is held in the basement of the plant, near the jockeys' quarters, in a film room far too small for the media contingent that jams into it after a successful Triple Crown. One last time Justify's connections, warm from the glow of his accomplishment and sweating from the excitement and the crowds, and now the closeness of this room, sat on a dais to try and put into words the meaning of their horse's achievements.

Baffert knew all too well the stakes of the day. Justify would either be remembered as just another good horse who near-missed immortality, or something far more.

"I wanted to see this horse…his name up there with those greats," he said, pointing to plaques on the wall of the first 12 Triple Crown winners. "It takes a great horse to win the Triple Crown."

Teo Ah Khing couldn't have written a better script for what he had been able to accomplish, and the portfolio he could now carry back to the powers that be in China that would help further his goals.

"We have 20 of our members here and they are on Cloud Nine, and so am I," he said. "We know the Triple Crown is not easy to achieve, and in three years in America, with great partners, we are indebted, and we are thankful."

WinStar's Kenny Troutt, normally calm, was sweating profusely and had expended even more energy rooting Justify on. "Seeing him come down that stretch, I mean, I was yelling and screaming and going crazy. It is a great blessing," he said.

Baffert was inevitably asked to compare his two Triple Crown winners, which he was still not willing to do publicly, saying, "It's like comparing your kids."

Smith, with just one Triple Crown winner on his docket, was far more direct: "Are you asking me? I think Justify's the greatest of all time. I just won the Triple Crown, man. He's my champion." After the laughter subsided, Smith grew serious. "There's a lot of pressure. I've ridden some good horses I thought could win the Derby, and they didn't. I'd won the Preakness and I've been blessed to win the Belmont a few times, but God gives you things when you're ready to handle them. And today I was ready. I felt good. I even took a nap, and that wouldn't have happened 10 or 20 years ago. I'd have been running through a wall or something. It's all the little things you learn over time."

Baffert then addressed the suddenness of Justify's presence on the scene and his lightning-fast ascension. "He was a walk-on," the trainer said. "He came in with all this raw talent and broke every curse there was. Everyone wants to get a horse like this; one of the most beautiful horses you'll ever see. He's just so tough, so imposing, and it's like he was telling them, 'Pass me to win.'"

None could.

17

CHANGE OF PLANS

DAYS AFTER HIS JUNE 16 PARADE AT CHURCHILL DOWNS AND the Kentucky Derby trophy presentations to Justify's owners and trainer, the Triple Crown winner flew back to his home base at Santa Anita Park. As he walked around the open area between Baffert's two barns there, a couple of dozen photographers and videographers pointed their equipment at the chestnut beauty, who seemed as fresh as when he had left California seven weeks earlier.

Baffert stood outside among them, giving interviews while admiring his Triple Crown winner. There had been a horse scale at Churchill Downs, but it was located clear across the stable area from Baffert's barn, and after the gravel incident, Baffert wasn't going to allow Justify to be walked anywhere there except to and from the racetrack. Finally, back in California, Justify was weighed. Through the entire Triple Crown experience, he had lost exactly three of his 1,260 pounds.

That he had maintained his condition was no secret to anyone even casually observing him. The horse looked ready to run again, anywhere, anytime. The plan, though, was to give him a break, and then race him once before pointing to the Breeders' Cup Classic, which was to be held November 3 back at Churchill Downs over a racetrack where Justify had already proven himself.

The race previous to the Breeders' Cup would likely be the Haskell Invitational, a grade 1 event at Monmouth Park in New Jersey and a race Baffert has dominated, winning it eight times in the last 17 runnings.

The owners of the other undefeated Triple Crown winner, Seattle Slew in 1977, found out the hard way that even racehorses who look invincible aren't. After his Belmont Stakes victory June 11, Slew was shipped to California to run in the Swaps Stakes against the wishes of his trainer Billy Turner. Hollywood Park increased the purse of the Swaps to $300,000 to lure Slew's connections, and in the July 3 Swaps, Slew failed to fire and finished fourth, 16 lengths behind J.O. Tobin.

So there was no hurry to bring Justify back into battle. Here again, Baffert would need to employ all his savvy to strike a compromise between not working Justify too hard while also not allowing him to become a couch potato. Justify galloped for a week at Santa Anita before Baffert and his staff noticed some filling on the inside of an ankle. After a period of rest, the swelling went away, and Justify returned to galloping.

"He moved well, but the filling came back up again," Baffert said. "He wasn't sore or anything, but there was something there, in an area of soft tissue, and if we did go on with him it may have torn or something. It's one of those things where you have to give them 90 days off, and we didn't have 90 days."

It is indisputable that commercial considerations today dominate horse racing, and that business decisions dwarf the sportsmanship that once carried the day when the family-owned stables ruled the roost. There is too much money at stake to take any undue chances with top potential breeding stock, and insurance costs alone can be determinant in how much a superior horse is raced. Top stud prospects today very rarely run past the age of

4, and many, including American Pharoah, are retired after their 3-year-old season.

This model, while financially sound, is a detriment to fans who have just become accustomed to following certain gifted runners and are beginning to attach themselves to the horses' fortunes. Early retirements discourage attracting and maintaining fans to the sport. That is the damning, indisputable truth. And a segment of racing's fan base, already buffeted about by the likely reality of losing money while gambling on horses, sees conspiracies behind every decision they do not like. The spiriting away of great horses from the racetrack and to stud duty is a ripe area for grousers. So a portion of the sport's followers would not believe Justify was actually injured unless they saw him walking with a cane. Early retirements are a frustrating situation for everyone who follows and loves the sport. But every sport today is also a business.

Perhaps Justify was so great that he could have come back after 90 days, train for a month, and still go on and win the Breeders' Cup Classic. Maybe he was that kind of superhorse. Just as likely, though, given that time frame, he would have mimicked the fortunes of Seattle Slew in the Swaps. It should be noted, however, that given Slew's era, he returned to the races as a 4-year-old and furthered his reputation as one of the greatest runners of all time.

Justify would not get that opportunity. On July 25, at the request of the colt's owners, Baffert announced Justify's retirement, and a subsequent news release had all the requisite quotes from his connections expressing praise, disappointment, and resignation. There is no logical reason to doubt the owners' initial plan was to run the horse twice more before retirement, nor is there any way to convince the conspiracy theorists of that.

Said Baffert a couple of months later, "You have a great horse with an issue, you don't want to mess around. It was bad enough with a bruised heel, you know what I mean? Unfortunately, a lot of people didn't believe our explanation, but I was looking forward to bringing him back to the races.

"With these kinds of horses, I just enjoy watching them run. I couldn't wait to watch him run again because he's so exciting. When you lead them out there, you know the crowds are crazy, they can't wait to see them, and you want to show them off. When we took Pharoah to the Haskell it was awesome. The crowds were waiting there and the other jockeys came out to see the race. Justify would have put on a show at the Haskell because from there on out, I would have told Mike to let him roll."

While his retirement ended Justify's potential to earn any more money as a racehorse, freezing his lifetime earnings at $3,798,000, it was just the briefest of setbacks for WinStar, China Horse Club, and SF Bloodstock, who would be splitting up their slices of Justify's $75-$85 million sale to Ashford Stud. It did, however, impact Jack Wolf, Sol Kumin, and their partners, whose interest in the colt was solely his racetrack earnings. If Justify were to win the Haskell and the Breeders' Cup Classic, approximately $3.6 million more in earnings would have been split up among those two groups, WinStar, and CHC, with Wolf and Kumin's groups each entitled to 15 percent of that haul.

However, on an original investment in Justify of between $300,000 and $400,000 each for their 15 percent stakes, both Wolf's and Kumin's groups had already made some money with the colt. Also, they shared in merchandising along the Triple Crown trail, such as when the Wheels Up private jet company paid to have its logo on Smith's pants leg in the Belmont Stakes. And, of course, they also experienced winning a Triple Crown.

Nevertheless, Justify's retirement marked the first time when the minority partners were at cross purposes with the colt's major stakeholders.

"There were a couple of decisions that were made that didn't agree with what we were trying to accomplish, which were grade 1 wins and purse earnings," noted Wolf. "Of course, we knew going in we weren't going to get to make those decisions. WinStar was the majority owner, and with the price Justify reportedly commanded, I can't disagree with the decision those guys made even though it didn't benefit our group.

"Obviously, with Justify, he was going to be worth more as a stallion prospect than taking the risk to run him again, and if I were in Elliott's shoes, I would have made the same decision. It just so happened we didn't benefit, but we were happy to be along for the ride. We had a unique time and we made money, at least until we try to buy all the trophies; that might put us in a hole."

Added Kumin, "The moment he crossed the finish line at the Belmont, my expectation was we would get to see him run two or three more times. We could have earned and it would have made it a better deal financially. But obviously the real money is in the breeding, which wasn't part of our deal.

"I was disappointed more than anything because I wanted to continue the journey. You get excited and involved, and then, bang, it's over. That makes it hard. I certainly didn't expect him to run at 4 because of how valuable he was when he won the Triple Crown. But the retirement was obviously much worse for Jack and me than it was for the other interests. For the first time, we weren't completely aligned."

In August, Justify again got on a plane and flew back to Kentucky. He took up temporary residence at WinStar Farm, which invited clients and guests to come out and see the Triple Crown winner. Ten days after his sale to Ashford was officially announced, Justify took the short van ride to his new home on September 17. Ashford announced his 2019 stud fee on September 23. It would cost $150,000 to breed to Justify in his first year at stud. Ashford had set American Pharoah's initial stud fee at $200,000 for the 2016 breeding season, but the market's reaction indicated the farm had overplayed its hand, and it wound up cutting deals off the announced price. Since 2016, American Pharoah's stud price has been listed as "private." Many of the breeders who sent mares to Pharoah have been well-rewarded, however. At the 2018 Keeneland September sale, 47 American Pharoah yearlings from his first crop to come to market sold for an average of $416,000.

At that 2018 Keeneland September yearling sale, John Gunther offered up Justify's half-brother (Thoroughbred half-siblings are out of the same mare but have different sires) by the stallion Will Take Charge. "I feel so strongly about this colt because he's got the same type of temperament as Justify," said Gunther. "He's big and strong and smart, and he knows he's a man among boys."

Buyers, however, knowing they were going to have to pay a hefty premium because of Justify's accomplishments, were hesitant to bid on the colt, hampered further by the fact Will Take Charge is a young stallion whose progeny have not yet made it to the racetrack. That is known in the business as being unproven. The colt only got two hits in the repository before entering the sales ring, and this time Gunther was determined to hold onto the yearling if he didn't get his price.

"Maybe people think lightning can't strike twice," he said. "But he is one of the best yearlings I've ever brought to the sale, and everybody is yawning and going to sleep. I was there the day he was born. I opened a door and saw him lying down, and his legs were from here to there; long. And I said to myself, 'We're not selling this one.' And I didn't even know it was Stage Magic's foal at that point. Plus Justify hadn't even run yet."

Gunther was good to his word. The final bid of $1.75 million didn't meet the reserve he put on the Will Take Charge colt, and so Gunther took Justify's half-brother back home to Glennwood.

In Justify's wake, a realignment took place among his connections that became evident at that September sale. SF Bloodstock dropped out of its buying partnership with WinStar Farm and China Horse Club. Instead, SF in partnership with a new entity formed by Jack Wolf named Starlight West, and with Sol Kumin as its third partner, bought 19 yearlings for a total of $9.3 million. The best of those yearlings will ultimately be ticketed for Baffert in California. The $9.3 million outlay made this new group the third-highest-ranked spenders at that sale.

Meantime, China Horse Club in partnership with Maverick Racing (Maverick is a name under which WinStar buys stock at auction) bought 12 yearlings for $6.1 million, ranking eighth on the list of leading buyers.

In the aftermath of the Noble Indy fiasco at the Belmont Stakes, owner Mike Repole pulled some 20 broodmares he had been boarding at WinStar off the farm. He also helped bankroll Lane's End Farm's deal to bring in new stallions West Coast and City of Light, who will both begin their stud careers there in 2019.

On October 4, it was announced that farm trainer Richard Budge, who oversaw the early conditioning of Justify at WinStar, was leaving the organization after more than a decade there.

On November 2 at Churchill Downs, on the undercard of the first day of the Breeders' Cup, a 2-year-old City Zip colt named Improbable, owned by WinStar, China Horse Club, and SF Racing, and trained by Baffert, won the Street Sense Stakes by 7¼ lengths. Following that race, SF sold its racing rights in the colt to Wolf's Starlight Racing. Improbable then won the grade 1 Cash Call Futurity on December 8, making him perfect in his first three starts. A $200,000 sales yearling, he has earned $269,520 from those first three races, and is a potential player in the 2019 classic races.

On November 3, on the undercard of the second day of the Breeders' Cup, Audible returned to the races for the first time since the Kentucky Derby, winning the Cherokee Run Stakes by two lengths for China Horse Club, WinStar, Starlight, and Sol Kumin's Head of Plains Partners.

That's a lot of action packed into one year. And a lot of changes.

...Tell Him your plans.

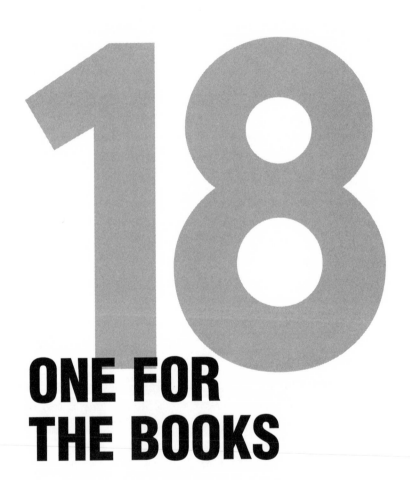

18
ONE FOR
THE BOOKS

JUSTIFY WILL HAVE EVERY OPPORTUNITY TO SUCCEED IN HIS career as a stallion. He will have the benefit of hooking up with top mares, and his first crops of progeny, should they look anything like him, will be pricey and wind up in the hands of the best connections. His name is likely to live on in pedigrees for generations.

As far as Justify's racing exploits go, all that remains is the question of where to place him within the sport's rich history. The Triple Crown conveys special status upon each of its 13 winners, and Justify's spot within the pantheon of great achievers seems destined to be balanced on the one side by his meteoric rise and on the other by his sudden departure.

Passion for certain horses shades opinion. While we believe Justify would have become one of the greatest horses of all time given the opportunity to prove himself over another season, that is admittedly pure speculation. So we conferred with a trio of the most respected Turf writers and experts of this era to discuss Justify's place in the annals of racing. Not surprisingly for a sport that exists because of people's disagreements over what they've seen and what they're about to see, opinions varied widely.

Ed Bowen is a former editor of *BloodHorse* magazine, for which he covered 22 Triple Crown seasons. He is also the author of 20 books on the sport and is a most-respected historian of racing. Steve Haskin, also of *BloodHorse*, has covered more than 30 Triple Crown seasons and has written a half dozen books on the sport, while Jay Hovdey is the executive columnist for *Daily Racing Form*, is an author of multiple books about racing, and has covered the sport for four decades. Both Haskin and Hovdey are enshrined in the Joe Hirsch Media Roll of Honor in the National Museum of Racing and Hall of Fame.

Hovdey preferred to take Justify's 3-year-old season in isolation rather than elevating it simply because the colt had not previously raced.

"I think it's meaningless to judge what a horse achieved at 3 based on how many times he ran at 2," he said. "I question the fact that his not racing at 2 was to his credit. Lucky Debonair won once at 2, bucked his shins, and came back and won the [1965] Derby. Is there a big difference between that and what Justify did? [Baffert] decided to wait a couple of weeks more to run him. Why get credit for that?

"On the one hand, no Triple Crown winner did any less than Justify. The positive spin is from the perspective of sheer compressed excitement. There's no other sport that has a two-month window where your superstar rises and then disappears. His racing career was a classic piece of work in that a 3-year-old was asked to do a lot in a short period of time in the lead-up to the Triple Crown. It was a real throwback-type of campaign.

"I was raised in an era when it was important for a horse to win any of the Triple Crown races. Do we as historians or analysts consider the highest achievement of a racehorse to be winning the Triple Crown? Anything else with Justify is speculative because all the other Triple Crown winners did something either before or after, and are elevated accordingly.

"In general, in today's game factors we once used to compare athletes from different eras have been stripped away; frequency of competition and carrying weight being two of them. We sound like old fogies today talking about a horse carrying 130 pounds in a handicap race. Today, management and economics have taken those things away from us.

"I think Justify leaves people scratching their heads a little bit. He appeared, he came, he saw, he conquered, and he split."

Bowen took a broader look by considering the various droughts between Triple Crown winners as a factor in how we view the individuals who conquered the three-race series.

"The shifting status of Triple Crown frequency complicates placing a horse in perspective," Bowen said. "Further, trying to do so in the immediate aftermath of his racing career is an inexact proposition. For Justify to have come along so soon after American Pharoah challenges us to sort out our emotions. Is a second Triple Crown somehow diminished in excitement and status because of proximity to a predecessor? The brevity of Justify's campaign adds another complicating element. But I think he must be seen in the light of what he did, not what one thinks he could have done given the good fortune of a more comprehensive menu of challenges."

At the end of last century, *BloodHorse* convened a panel of racing historians to rank the top 100 American racehorses of the 20th century. Triple Crown winners Secretariat and Citation were ranked second and third, respectively (behind Man o' War), with Count Fleet, Seattle Slew, Affirmed, and War Admiral all ranked in the top 13. Omaha was tabbed the lowest of the Triple Crown winners at number 61.

"With a vague sense of needing to apologize to Justify," said Bowen, "I would tentatively group him in the lower tier among the exalted population of Triple Crown winners. That comes with the proviso of retaining the right of re-evaluation as time works its own influences. If decades pass without another undefeated Triple Crown winner or—perish the thought—without any Triple Crown winner, Justify will take on a more exalted persona. What must be uppermost in thought, of course, is that being in the group of 13 is in itself a lofty status."

While Hovdey looked at Justify's 3-year-old season in a vacuum, Haskin found historical perspective useful in placing the colt's accomplishments in context. He noted that the 12 previous Triple Crown winners entered the Belmont Stakes with an average of almost 14 career starts that began, on average, a year earlier than their Belmont Stakes. Justify carried five lifetime starts over only a 3½-month period into that race, shorter by five months than the next shortest span, Seattle Slew's 8½ months.

Before Justify's Belmont, Haskin wrote, "Justify will be trying to read *War and Peace* in a day; play Brahms' Second Piano Concerto in five minutes. After what we've seen, can anyone say for certain he can't do it?"

Haskin, a devout racing historian who takes precedent to heart, marveled at the colt's accomplishments when compared to all who had come before him.

"For a horse to cram six races, four grade 1 victories, and a sweep of the Triple Crown into such a short period of time is unimaginable," he noted. "Horses just don't do that. And he did it racing on three fast tracks, two sloppy tracks, and one muddy track, while winning his six races at six different distances from seven furlongs to a mile and a half.

"He defied all logic. Horses, especially those with no racing foundation, are not supposed to be subjected to such a grueling schedule and get stronger after each race. He rewrote the history book, accomplishing feats not even the all-time greats could come close to."

Those feats included:

- Becoming the first horse in 136 years to win the Kentucky Derby without having raced as a 2-year-old.
- Becoming the second horse in 103 years to win the Derby with only three career starts.
- Running the fastest (early) winning fractions in the history of the Kentucky Derby.

Haskin noted that Justify was part of a North American foal crop that numbered about 23,000 Thoroughbreds. When Sir Barton became the first Triple Crown winner, in 1919, there were 1,665 horses in his crop; in Gallant Fox's year (1930), there were 5,137; and when Citation won it in 1948, 8,434. Although there were 32,114 in Affirmed's crop (3-year-olds of 1978), the Kentucky Derby was then open to lesser horses, unlike today when they must qualify in top graded stakes.

Haskin also pointed out that the previous 12 Triple Crown winners faced an average of 4.6 opponents in the Belmont Stakes, with Count Fleet, Whirlaway, Omaha, Gallant Fox, and Sir Barton all facing just two or three foes. Secretariat and Affirmed ran against four opponents in the race, and none of the Triple Crown winners had faced more than seven competitors until nine lined up against Justify.

Acknowledging the trend of horses racing less frequently over the past 20 years, Haskin sees Justify as the ultimate personification of that movement.

"History told us that winning the Kentucky Derby two and a half months after his debut race was a pipe dream," Haskin stated. "Sweeping the Triple Crown 16 weeks after his first race was unthinkable. In the context of history, it was almost laughable.

"Sure, you had a feeling that one of these years a special horse would come along and rewrite history by accomplishing feats never before accomplished; a horse who would stamp his name in racing lore. But for the historians—those who rely on the past to help dictate the present—they needed to see it done.

"In many ways, Justify has made us shut the history books for good. He has shown us there is nothing unattainable, regardless of what history tells us. He made us realize there are no longer worlds that cannot be conquered.

"That makes Justify one of the most important horses of our time. It is too early to know for sure just how great a horse he is, but he has surely brought about change, mainly in the way we think. And there is something extremely profound in that. From now on, whenever we see a horse trying to do something that has never been done before, or has rarely been done, we will think of Justify and what he accomplished.

"Forget speed figures and huge margins of victory. Justify is all about winning and doing so in a remarkably short period of time."

My lasting impression of Justify begins with my first impression of him. If only you could have seen how he filled up his stall, a superstar athlete just beginning to realize the immensity of his talent. If you could have seen him emerge from quarters and stride to the racetrack to do battle. If you saw the power in motion of a competitor who refused to be defeated…

Of the thousands of racehorses one sees as a chronicler of the sport, once in a long while you get a special feeling about one. You're not always right, but often enough to trust your judgment, you are. A.P. Indy. Phone Chatter. Bernardini. Songbird. Justify fit with them right off the jump. Yet through injury or the lure of the stud, all left the racetrack prematurely. That each left their mark in abbreviated moments in the spotlight is to be celebrated, yet balanced against the lamentation of what could have been.

Like the great runner and stallion A.P. Indy, Justify didn't need to win his races by huge margins that may have seemed more impressive to some. But most importantly, he did need to win. He had the heart, the courage, the mind, the legs, and the motor. He was a perfect racehorse in deed and in looks, the finest physical specimen of a Thoroughbred we've seen in two decades of covering the sport. And while the legendary track announcer Trevor Denman often intones that racing "is not a beauty contest," it is also true that only a certain kind of horse can withstand the rigors of training, especially as practiced by Bob Baffert, who will test his runners in the morning before unleashing them in the afternoon. Those qualifications are usually met by big-boned, muscular horses.

At the 2018 Keeneland yearling sale, Baffert was looking at a potential purchase in the barn area. After a brief once-over, he thanked the handler and watched him take the yearling back to his stall. "I've never led one over for a grade 1 race that looked like that," Baffert said, crossing the yearling off his list.

Whether a couple more races would have eased the concerns of Justify's detractors is hard to say. American Pharoah ran three times after his Belmont Stakes victory, winning twice. He took the Breeders' Cup Classic over mostly weak competition, the exception being Honor Code, a confirmed closer ill-equipped to deal with Pharoah's front-running style. That victory elevated American Pharoah since he did defeat older horses in the race, but American Pharoah, it seems to us, will be likely far better known as the first Triple Crown winner in 37 years than he will as one of the 10 greatest racehorses in history.

In our opinion—and that is all it is—there was more upside to Justify. In the current economics of horse racing, however, neither an American Pharoah nor a Justify will get to prove himself over time. Champion-caliber colts who are today kept in training through their 4-year-old season either bloomed late or had other circumstances attached to them.

California Chrome, a Kentucky Derby and Preakness winner, carried obscure-enough breeding so as not to be immediately attractive to major stud farms following his 3-year-old season. Then, his 4-year-old campaign was mismanaged and undercut by injury, leading to his racing again at 5. Gun Runner and Arrogate, who each ran at 4, both came on to excel after their crop's Triple Crown series.

We are at a juncture in horse racing where we might get to know an outstanding colt as a late 2-year-old through his 3-year-old season, but not for much longer than that if he has proven to be precocious and is well-pedigreed. Justify took that condensed schedule to its extreme, but in his excellence he is a poster boy for today's economic reality, not an exception to the reigning rule.

As Hovdey noted, the factors by which great horses have historically been judged have changed as radically in racing as "dinosaur statistics" have in sports such as baseball, today having been replaced in the minds of a new breed by cyber stats that seem a foreign world to traditionalists.

No statistic, though, measures intangibles like courage, heart, and the will to win. Anyone who has actually competed successfully in athletics knows more about those factors than anyone sitting at a computer. How to measure the greatness of a horse? We can utilize graphs of speed figures and pages of race records and quality of competition. And then it is still left to each of us to offer our opinion in an attempt to state the unknowable.

For his trainer, Justify stands as a most-significant confirmation of greatness. Baffert's status as a worthy Hall of Famer had already been achieved and validated, but a second Triple Crown winner raises him into another conversation, that of greatest trainer of all time.

Like a line drive hit directly at a center fielder, it is hardest to judge events that are unfolding in front of us day-to-day. Sixty-five at the time of Justify's Triple Crown, Baffert hopefully has many seasons still in front of him to burnish his record. A singular achievement can always be viewed as a fluke. Although Billy Turner (Seattle Slew) and Lucien Laurin (Secretariat) were fine trainers who enjoyed notable careers, there is no doubt that one horse would appear in the first sentence of each of their epitaphs. Perhaps two, if Riva Ridge is placed in the first line for Laurin.

Baffert must be looked at, at this juncture in his career, alongside Ben Jones and James "Sunny Jim" Fitzsimmons as the elite of the elite. A second Triple Crown winner eliminates any doubt as to his rightful placement. It would be foolish to attempt to predict the future, but from here it appears one would have to go a ways out on the horizon to see somebody soon surpassing Baffert's 15 Triple Crown race victories, a number that figures to swell further. SF Bloodstock, Starlight West, and Sol Kumin's plans to send their best horses his way is illustrative of a trend among top owners around the country. Baffert only figures to attract more of the finest stock and get stronger in the immediacy, frightening for his competitors considering Justify marks the trainer's fourth consecutive 3-year-old champion.

But it is also Baffert's four Breeders' Cup Juvenile winners (including 2018's Game Winner), five Breeders' Cup Sprint winners, three consecutive Breeders' Cup Classic winners, and his ability to train horses like Game On Dude and Hoppertunity to graded stakes victories as 7-year-olds that stamp his excellence in all dirt divisions and with all manner of horses. The smart money has Baffert eclipsing most all standing records related to training in the Triple Crown races. He is one victory behind Ben Jones for Kentucky Derby wins and is tied with R. Wyndham Walden with seven Preakness wins (Walden's all came between 1875 and 1888).

The only Triple Crown mark seemingly out of his reach is James G. Rowe Sr.'s eight Belmont Stakes victories.

His peers certainly appreciate his skills. "It was a real experience for me as a former trainer to see how he handled the superstar status of this horse, with the media and everything else," said Walden. "Bob has an amazing ability to keep it all in perspective, keep it light, and also pay attention to the details. He's able to shrug off what doesn't matter and focus on what does. It isn't easy. All the travel, all kinds of details you have to be on top of when every day counts. And as you go through it, the pressure builds, the intensity builds."

Added Chad Brown, "To take a horse that never started at 2, have that many races so close together…I know Bob gives the credit to the horse, but it takes somebody at the helm to call all the shots, especially after the Derby when things didn't go as planned. For Bob to have the focus to call all the right shots and get that horse through the Triple Crown is an amazing training job. The best I've ever seen in my time following horse racing."

That line drive is heading right at us and deserves to be appreciated in real time.

Justify's ultimate place in the pecking order of our Thoroughbred heroes is dynamic, and will no doubt undergo change as our thought patterns evolve based on events yet to come. The evaluations and memories of him from those closely connected to the colt are far more settled.

"He wasn't a mean horse," said Baffert, "but my little pony who always went with him to and from the track, every day he walked with his ears pinned like he was thinking, 'This guy can eat me at any moment he wants.' But he didn't. It was like walking around a great white shark. You could tell that pony always felt intimidated.

"But that's the kind of horse Justify is. I've never had a horse that, wherever he was—the barn, the track—he was imposing, like he owned the place. He strolled around like whatever the job, it was no big deal."

Kumin first met the horse just before the Santa Anita Derby, and Justify made a lasting impression. "He just had this way about him," Kumin said. "He looked different than the other horses; bigger, stronger, more confident. Like a man among boys. After the race I remember flying home with my son and telling him, 'This is a special horse.'"

Said SF Bloodstock's Tom Ryan, "He was literally the experience of a lifetime, and we feel privileged to have been a part of history. We couldn't say it any better than the tribute David Hains paid to his great galloper Kingston Town: 'He gave us the stars. He didn't need to give us the moon, too, but he did.'"

"Bob said he's never had a horse with such perfect conformation," noted Jill Baffert. "Justify is just so big and flashy. Pharoah was beautiful, but more unassuming. When Justify came out he was like a beautiful shiny copper penny, and he had his little forelock. They were both my babies. You couldn't ask for more in racing or life."

Brown, who has every chance to take up the mantle of best contemporary trainer if and when Baffert relinquishes it, said, "You know, for two legs of the Triple Crown—in the Derby with Good Magic and the Belmont with Gronkowski—at the quarter pole, I felt very, very good about my horses' chances to beat Justify. I thought my horses had very good trips and had every chance, but they just couldn't get there. Justify did all the running; ran every pole. Nobody gave him anything. So the conclusion is that Justify was just too good.

"It's horse racing. And enough time has passed where I've accepted all of it. There are probably other people in other [horse] divisions who regret that I had special horses at the time that they couldn't get by. You run into a horse of a lifetime…"

19
BACK TO THE BEGINNING

AS NOON APPROACHES ON A RAW LATE-NOVEMBER CENTRAL Kentucky day, Justify is brought out from his stone stallion quarters at Ashford Stud for a quick photoshoot. An orange halter crown cover made of fleece runs over the back of his head, and he is full of himself. He's much more interested in biting the chain of his lead shank and challenging his handler than he is in posing for a photograph.

He has gained weight in preparation for his upcoming work, and resides in the in-between stage of athlete on the one hand and stallion on the other. He becomes studdish within five minutes, indicating he will perform capably in his upcoming job. This portion of his life will last another two and a half months, until he begins his time as a breeding animal in mid-February.

One year ago, he had just begun breezing for Mike Marlow at Los Alamitos, and Bob Baffert had just gotten his first look at this chestnut dynamo. It has been a dizzying ride, if not for Justify, then for all the humans who came to share his orbit.

THE SEASON'S FIRST SNOWFALL blankets the farmland along the five miles of McCracken Pike between the small town of Versailles and Glennwood Farm. As you travel west, on the right side of the road are side entrances to Stonestreet Farm, the birth-place of Good Magic; and to Ashford Stud.

The area's limestone-rich land is fertile and proven to nurture young equine lives. The pike is dotted with a half dozen horse operations. Glennwood is a classic farm. Because it is non-commercial, there are no fancy cupolas or copper accents up on the roofs of the barns. Everything is functional and well-maintained. The ribbons of roadway that curve through the pastures connecting the barns give no grief to auto axles. Ten staffers maintain the 440 acres, two dozen broodmares, and the foals, weanlings, and yearlings for John and Tanya Gunther. Outside one of the farm's main gates, Conrado Campos and a co-worker clear tree limbs felled by a night's ice storm.

The dean of Glennwood's equine handlers, Campos, from Guanajuato, Mexico, has more than 20 years invested at the farm, foaling out and raising babies. He is dressed for the bruising cold in which he works, and the chilling drafts blowing through Barn 5 don't ease until he enters the barn's tack room, which turns out to be uncomfortably hot due to an active wall heater. He peels his jacket's throat guard away from his neck, slightly ill at ease speaking with a digital recorder in front of him. His English is not fluent, but his meaning is crystal clear as he speaks of the farm's most famous graduate.

"It is hard to know as a baby whether a horse is going to go do something special," Campos says, "but when Justify was a baby in the field he was the best one there. He always wanted to play when the others didn't feel like it; he had a lot of energy and was happy all the time."

Told that everyone who had touched the colt along the way commented on how smart he was, Campos nods. "He showed that whenever he went to the track," he said. "He was so relaxed, like he knows where he's going and knows what he's doing. Watching him on TV, he made it look like it was nothing. No nervousness. Get to the track ready to go.

"Nothing I have seen since is quite like him. But there is hope."

A few minutes' drive over to Barn 1 finds Ricardo Lopez working around the soon-to-be yearlings, preparing them for their late-morning turnout to the farm's paddocks. People like Campos and Lopez form the backbone of the horse industry in North America. They are the workers who show up, often seven days a week and through any and all weather, at farms and race-tracks to handle and care for these animals, who know them the best, and whose love for them makes Thoroughbred racing pos-sible. They toil away largely in obscurity, and in many cases for operations whose victories, if any, are small ones, accomplished far away from the glare of spotlights and national television.

At Glennwood, though, a special air permeates. Each one of the workers here has had a hand in developing greatness. They know dreams come true and prayers get answered. Here, there is an assured feeling and a confidence. It is just another morning of work, like hundreds of others this season. But it has been a season unlike any other.

Lopez, with jet-black hair and a sharply shaped beard, has five years at Glennwood prepping yearlings for auction as well as working the sales. He handled Justify enough to know his nature.

"He loved doing whatever task was in front of him, whether it was going on the [electric] walker here or being shown at the sale," Lopez says. "He was always full of himself, but he let you do whatever you needed to do with him without bothering you."

Lopez has high hopes for Justify's yearling half-brother, the Will Take Charge colt who is back at Glennwood. In him, Lopez sees the past and possibly the future.

"He is actually a little taller than Justify, but the same in that he stands out among the others," he said. "And as soon as he gets to the field and you turn him loose, he runs to one of the corners and rolls in the dirt, the same as Justify did. That is pretty awesome, to see him do just what his brother used to do."

Lopez watched the Triple Crown races from his home. "When he came out of the gate in the Kentucky Derby, I told my wife, 'This is his race. He's winning this race,'" Lopez says. "Same at the Belmont Stakes. I was yelling, 'Keep going, boy.' And then when he won I broke down and cried. Seeing that horse do it all in 111 days, and I know him since he was a baby…it was like having a newborn. I always wanted to be part of an incredible horse, and I thank Tanya for letting me work with him, and to work here. I love what I do, and Justify is the best thing that has happened in my life with horses."

When Justify arrived at Ashford in September, Ashford's people graciously invited the Glennwood team to partake in the welcome festivities, and the Glennwood staff took the short drive over to see him, the first time they had laid eyes on Justify since he left the Keeneland sale two years earlier headed for WinStar Farm.

"He was always muscled, but at Ashford he was fantastically impressive," Lopez says. "I've not seen a better-looking horse than him."

It's time for Lopez to return to work. He and office manager Lindsay Wilson confer on a game plan for getting the farm's yearlings and weanlings to their paddocks.

"Yes," says Lopez, "now we take the next Triple Crown winner out to the field."

ACKNOWLEDGMENTS

The author wishes to thank the following for their insights and cooperation: Bob and Jill Baffert, Mike Smith, John and Tanya Gunther, Steve Haskin, Ed Bowen, Jay Hovdey, Larry Collmus, Richard Budge, David Hanley, Ricardo Lopez, Conrado Campos, Lindsay Wilson, Elliott Walden, Jack Wolf, Sol Kumin, Humberto Gomez, Steve Byk, Tim Layden, Rick Samuels, Michael Blowen, Gary Young, Mike Marlow, Tom Ryan, Rick Hammerle, Chad Brown, John Moynihan, D. Wayne Lukas, Mike Pegram, Martin Panza, Gerrie Sturman, Ronald Goldfarb, and special thanks to Paul Volponi for his inspiration.